On Site

Preparing Middle Level Teachers Through Field Experiences

Deborah A. Butler
Mary A. Davies
Thomas S. Dickinson

NATIONAL MIDDLE SCHOOL ASSOCIATION

nmsa

NATIONAL MIDDLE SCHOOL ASSOCIATION

The authors of this report are all highly qualified to deal with this important topic. All have been actively involved in middle level teacher education for many years. Deborah A. Butler is Associate Professor and Director of Teacher Education at Wabash College in Crawfordsville, Indiana; Mary A. Davies is Assistant Professor, Department of Education and Professional Development at Western Michigan University in Kalamazoo. Thomas S. Dickinson is Editor, *Middle School Journal,* National Middle School Association, Columbus, Ohio and former professor in North Carolina, Illinois, and Georgia.

The Association is grateful to these professional leaders for their initiative in developing this ground-breaking monograph. Appreciation is also expressed to the contributing authors, C. Kenneth McEwin and J. Pat Knight of Appalachian State University, Boone, North Carolina; Larry M. Putbrese of St. Cloud State University, Minnesota; Edward N. Brazee and John W. Pickering of the University of Maine, Orono; Jerry Moore and Tom Oppewal of the University of Virginia, Charlottesville; and Cliff P. Bee and Linda Kramer of San Diego State University, California.

Printed in the United States of America by Panaprint, Inc., P.O. Box 10297, Macon, GA 31297

ISBN 1-56090-059-8

Dedication

to
C. Kenneth McEwin

for his leadership and dedication to the cause of middle school teacher education. His tireless efforts have been a beacon to those who believe that young adolescents are best served by those who are specifically prepared to teach them.

Table of Contents

Foreword

The NATIONAL MIDDLE SCHOOL ASSOCIATION has played a key role in efforts to correct the long-standing need for teacher education programs and state certification specifically designed for the middle level. In 1979 an ad hoc committee was appointed and directed to prepare a statement addressing this issue. The committee, chaired by Tom Gatewood, presented its report in 1980. The Board of Trustees accepted the position paper and established a standing committee to institute action on the paper's recommendation. In 1984, in order to expand the Association's efforts, William M. Alexander and C. Kenneth McEwin were asked to prepare a more comprehensive statement. Their report, which included the original position paper as an appendix, was officially adopted and was published in 1986. Wide distribution of the pamphlet followed.

Two years later *Preparing to Teach at the Middle Level* was published. This monograph, also written by Alexander and McEwin, was the first comprehensive treatment of this topic ever published—and it remains the only such document. It provided guidelines and descriptions of existing programs. Then most recently the Association's Professional Preparation and Certification Committee in a highly intensive and thoroughly professional process developed the first-ever middle level teacher preparation guidelines. With guidelines for both basic and advanced programs, these standards have become the official National Middle School Association/National Council for the Accreditation of Teacher Education position on middle level teacher education. All institutions seeking NCATE accreditation for any middle level program must submit their curriculum folios to *NMSA*'s Folio Review Board.

One of the main sections in the new middle level standards deals with what is probably the most critical element in a teacher education program, field experiences. Called for correctly are early *and* continuing involvement with middle level schools. This monograph, *On Site: Preparing Middle Level Teachers Through Field Experiences*, adds needed specificity concerning various ways field experiences can be organized and operated. It is rich in detail and demonstrates the variety of collaborative approaches that can achieve the needed involvement in school sites.

The issuance of *On Site* comes at a propitious time. Teacher education institutions all across the country are now moving rapidly to provide the professional preparation needed to match the burgeoning number of middle schools. Because the middle level is a relatively recent focal point in education, many collegiate institutions have no faculty member adequately conversant in this rapidly expanding educational reform effort. Needed, then, is the type of basic information provided herein. The authors and editors are all experienced middle level teachers and teacher educators. Their obvious knowledge of sound middle school practice and of reality is evident.

In the years just ahead hundreds and hundreds of teachers will be completing recently established middle level certification programs. They will take their places on faculties, not as retreads, but as *bona fide* middle level professionals. The programs they complete will be better for the guidance and examples offered in this pioneering publication and the middle school youngsters they teach will receive more effective educational experiences. Every teacher education institution involved in middle level programs will find much of value in this monograph.

John H. Lounsbury
Publications Editor, *NMSA*

Part I

The Power of Good Middle Level Field Experiences

The Power of Good Middle Level Field Experiences

In their 1988 monograph, *Preparing to Teach at the Middle Level*, Alexander and McEwin reiterate the statement of "essential elements of a middle level teacher education program" taken from the 1986 National Middle School Association position paper, *Professional Certification and Preparation for the Middle Level*. Comprised of five areas, the document includes as a fifth necessity "early and continuing field experiences in good middle schools" (p. 48).

Even more recently, *Turning Points: Preparing American Youth for the 21st Century* (1989), a document prepared by the Carnegie Council on Adolescent Development, echoed this need: "Teachers for the middle grades are specifically prepared to teach young adolescents" (p. 36). In addition, the document added: "Above all else, prospective middle grade teachers need to understand adolescent development through courses and direct experience in middle grade schools" (p. 59).

In the profession of teacher education at any level, there is no quarrel about the necessity and inherent validity of early field experiences and student teaching; the rationale, the theoretical and practical bases for meaningful field experiences have long been identified and supported by both research and professional wisdom. Middle school experiences are no exception.

The many benefits of any field experience include these two:

1. Field experiences are "life laboratories;" the experiences and subsequent reflections help build cognitive structures necessary for adapting to the teaching role. In other words, field experiences provide students opportunities to practice key concepts.

2. Participants and their supervisors provide a continuing link between school and college/university, at its best a two-way street where new ideas and new realities enliven both school and college.

These and other benefits can accrue from any elementary, any high school, or any middle school experience. And yet, they, and a wealth of other benefits, are gained best from experiences derived from the context of one's intended level of teaching. For example, no professional educator would dream of placing prospective elementary teachers for their early experience or student teaching in a high school setting. Nor would it cross our minds to train our high school teachers solely with elementary participation. Yet, this non-contextual kind of experience, including student teaching, is often the norm for those who become middle level teachers. Because some teachers did not intend initially to become middle level teachers, or because their programs responded to state certifications (like K-8 or 5-12 or 7-12), their middle level exposure was de-emphasized or even skipped over. The result for many teachers' backgrounds is the same—they do not build experientially a cognitive structure for future teaching in the middle grades. They do not get that fifth basic or essential, the "early and continuing field experiences in good middle schools."

But there are other reasons, beyond this "contextual" argument, why middle level experiences are essential, why they are irreplaceable by any other kind of experience. Some are "professional" reasons; some are more "practical."

Special professional reasons include the following three.

1. We can, as teachers, administrators, guidance people, and college supervisors, help prospective teachers verify their learnings of unique developmental issues for young adolescents by placing these candidates "among them." We can also, by placing them in "good middle schools," afford them the opportunity to see how school structures (curriculum, buildings, schedules) can be shaped to encourage both adults and adolescents to grow and learn best.

2. Although more undergraduate teaching candidates come to us with

personal backgrounds that include experience in contemporary middle grades settings, many still do not. Complicating this, many prospective middle level teachers are drawn from the ranks of older people returning for initial certification and degrees, or are returning teachers recertifying at the middle level. We still have a clientele which needs the best possible ideals and models of teachers and programs as part of their education.

3. We need particularly field experiences at the middle level because our prospective teachers must come to appreciate the unique developmental issues confronting young adolescents. Nearly as important, these novices ought to see exemplary teachers of middle grades students. They need to be exposed early to the special role definition of the good middle grades teacher, that is, the teacher who is cooperative, creative, a positive encourager of learning, someone who is fully knowledgeable about early adolescence and allows this knowledge to influence practice effectively. Such master teachers need to be seen, and to have their images imprinted on future teachers.

Practical reasons exist, too, for developing and maintaining middle level field experiences.

1. Involvement in real middle schools with real middle school kids dispels the negative stereotype many prospective teachers have of these students. Sometimes teaching candidates remember with pain their own early adolescence. Sometimes, they pick up the snide comments and asides which demean teachers and students at the "junior" high level. Wherever the stereotype comes from, it is often there and must be acknowledged as a barrier to teacher recruitment. Good, thought-provoking field experiences can provide an antidote to this situation; they can allow a realistic yet open-minded view to emerge, a willingness to entertain the challenges and to experience the unique opportunities available in middle level education. If good field experiences are coupled with good middle school advocates in teacher education classrooms and in kid's classrooms, we can recruit potentially excellent prospective teachers.

2. Finally, providing field experiences for the study of middle level education accents the visibility of "the middle" and its teacher education component. If more schools and colleges provided separate and distinct field programs, a necessary statement about the importance of these schools, these teachers, and these students would be made.

In the next section of this monograph we provide descriptions of several collaborative efforts between schools and colleges which accent the importance of middle school field experiences. The first four models deal with ways in which the institutions involved structure pre-student teaching field experiences at the middle level. The last three offer models for structuring student teaching.

The first example provides a view of a very early field experience component for Wabash College freshmen and sophomores, one which offers observation and participation integrated with computer-assisted instruction on the developmental characteristics of young adolescents. The second is a description of an intensive middle school level shadow study experience required of all middle grades teaching majors at Georgia Southern University.

Following these are two examples of "immersion" early field experiences. Appalachian State University's intern teaching experience is an intensive pre-student teaching experience designed to allow students to apply recently learned theory and strategies in a teaching practicum. The Early Adolescent Block at St. Cloud State University, described next, integrates fully its pre-service teachers in site-based middle level teaching.

Middle grades student teaching experiences vary widely. The University of Maine offers a "multiple" site opportunity for student teaching within its four-year program design. Two other student teaching models described here illustrate middle level practica within five-year programs. The University of Virginia's five year program accommodates the beginning professional who desires training and experience at the middle level, while San Diego State University's intense three semester sequence includes a site-based intern teaching year as the culmination of its teaching program.

Taken together, the seven examples of field experience options presented suggest a range of valid field experience possibilities. They are a few of the many realities which have been envisioned and can be implemented in various program settings where professionals strive collaboratively to educate "essentially" our future middle level teachers.

References

Alexander, W. M., & McEwin, C. K. (1988). *Preparing to teach at the middle level.* Columbus, OH: National Middle School Association.

Carnegie Council on Adolescent Development. (1989). *Turning points: Preparing American youth for the 21st century.* New York: Carnegie Corporation.

National Middle School Association. (1986). *Professional certification and preparation for the middle level: A position paper.* Columbus, OH: Author.

Part II

Models of Early Field Experiences at the Middle Level

Early Observations
of Developmental Characteristics
# of Young Adolescents

Deborah A. Butler

Wabash College, a small, liberal arts college for men, was founded in 1832, in part to "train teachers." It has been active in undergraduate teacher education ever since. Although most students prepare to teach high school, some eventually go into middle level teaching and all receive, as undergraduates, observation and participation experiences in middle grades.

Pre-service field experiences at Wabash College begin early and extend throughout the student's undergraduate years, culminating with student teaching. Most students observe and teach in classrooms within the three districts in the surrounding county. The college is located in a small community in a predominantly rural area. There is a long history of close working relationships among county and city teachers, administrators, and the Wabash education program.

Overview of the field experience program

The overarching intent of all field experiences is to move the young novice from reflective observation to more involved, yet still reflective participation as he journeys from the student's side of the desk to the teacher's. As either freshmen or sophomores, prospective Wabash teachers engage for a semester in the first field practicum, **Educational Psychology 1**, where participating students witness the stages of human development by direct observation. Later, as juniors studying the sociological, historical, and philosophical bases of American education, the focus of field experiences shift to a critical examination of various types of alternative schools and diverse student populations. As juniors beginning to learn methodology, observation gives way to participation and refocuses on the microcosm of the classroom and the interactions of students, teachers, curriculum—the teaching-learning processes themselves. These second semester juniors learn and apply their planning skills as part of a two-week-long teaching episode as the culmination of the course. As seniors about to enter student teaching, about 90% are placed for participatory hours within classrooms where they will student teach.

Focus on the first field experience—the middle grades

Educational Psychology 1 is an experience composed of coordinated classroom observations at three levels of schooling (elementary, middle, and high school). Specific observation modules designed to engage each participant in critical analysis of the total environment of school combine with computer-assisted instruction on young and older adolescent development, and discussion/de-briefing groups, to complete each level of experience. The structure of each mini-unit within the practicum could be diagrammed as such:

Computer-assisted instruction on human development

$\updownarrow$

Directed observation/participation in schools

$\updownarrow$

De-briefing of practicum experience

The goal of this first experience is to observe learners' human development patterns throughout various phases of the school years. This instructional pattern repeats itself three times in the practicum: when students observe children in K-5 classrooms; when they are with young adolescents in grades 6-8; and when they observe in grades 9-12.

Preparation for the middle level experience

The middle level part of this experience begins in the college classroom after the K-5 experience is completed during the first third of the semester. During the discussion of their observations at the elementary level, college students and supervisor begin to turn the focus toward the young adolescent learners whom they will observe next. Questions like, "How might 6-8th graders priorities differ from 4-5th graders?" or "What do you expect to see distinctively different from the elementary level in those

6-8th grade classrooms?" or "What differences in students do you expect?" serve to generate some hypotheses. Students leave this session with directions to complete within the next week a part of the computer instruction on younger and older adolescent changes.

The computer-assisted instruction that students complete consists of five separate modules developed cooperatively by the Psychology Department and the Education Program at Wabash College. The first three modules are required before the middle level visit. They focus on the physical, intellectual, and moral developmental changes that begin in early adolescence. Final sections deal with social and societal expectations and problems of the adolescent. These are completed before the final one-third of the experience at the high school level.

Since the disks with the five modules are checked out to individual students, they work at their own paces during the week before the middle level observations begin. Computer disks are returned to the Education Office after each user completes the required parts. The computers themselves are accessible in several labs on campus as well as in several fraternity and dormitory houses. Although the modules employ a basic read-question-answer format, questions were specifically developed at the application levels or above on Bloom's *Taxonomy* to challenge students' thinking. Each disk houses files for the student user, recording his responses to questions. Printouts from the disks are easily obtainable for instructor and student perusal.

In the meantime, placements are made at a local middle school. Administrators and teachers usually involved with the middle level component of the early field observation teach at Tuttle Middle School in Crawfordsville, Indiana. In 1986, Tuttle made a transition to a 6-8 middle school with team organization, advisories, and interdisciplinary instruction. Initially placements are made through either the principal or assistant principal, but increasingly, the placement is given to individual team leaders, who then, within the team, discuss the program of participation for the one or two students they receive for the two-week practicum (10 periods of classroom contact). A description of each participant's assigned team and visitation periods is returned to the college supervisor's office before the college student finishes his week's review of adolescent development.

Since middle school assignments arrive back on campus the week of computer-assisted instruction, students emerge from the computer sequence ready to begin the two week participation with a team of teachers and students. Participants report to the school at their appointed times to meet the principals and then to meet team leaders and team teachers.

Most teachers integrate the participant into classroom activity in similar ways. Says one: "I have a chair ready for him beside my desk. I explain the type of class he is observing and give him a copy of all books and lesson plans for the day. I always introduce the student observer to my class as 7th grade students are naturally curious. I also put our visitor in front of the room on purpose. If I did not, the class would spend the entire hour turned in their seats!" Another adds: "...Time and situation available, the observer may be permitted to work one on one with an individual student."

Most teachers take as a primary goal helping a participant remember his subject, that is, the "...nature of middle school students in general."

The observation/participation process

While teachers set their own agendas with the observers and provide them with participatory opportunities, the students also select two intensive assignments which relate directly to material on development just studied and to experiences with young adolescents. Specific assignments are drawn from George and Lawrence's *Handbook for Middle School Teaching* (1982), and emphasize physical and intellectual development of the young adolescent learner. Participants must choose one assignment of the two related to physical characteristics of young adolescents, and one from the two designed to provide insight into intellectual development.

Teachers know that the students have some specific observations to complete and describe in their observation logs, but they know, too, that participation hours remain after these are completed, and that involvement is encouraged. In fact, during the most recent term, participants taught mini-lessons to young adolescents, thus increasing the level of participation. If, however, the participant and teacher do not find ways to involve the participant directly during the two week experience, a reflective observation form provided in each participant's log guides his observation. Often student speculation from these more "open" observation sequences allows interesting insights to appear in later discussions on campus.

The total range of possible and required components yields some important insights and often verifies the knowledge base participants begin to acquire during the sessions with the computer units. One Wabash College student notes about physical development: "I had always thought that the elementary group would be more energetic, but to me, the students seem much more active/hyperactive. Since most of the students at middle school are changing physically in ways they don't understand, they translate these changes into an almost endless supply of energy. This is why they can't even sit still for five minutes."

Another's comments substantiate this observation: "The patterns of physical activity can be compared to a roller coaster ride. Attention seemed to be there, then slowly fade out, then come back in again all through the class...." And later: "They all exhibited tense energy, which is why I focused on attention span for most of my journal."

A freshman participant focused on biological development characteristics and noted that: "...it was evident that the females in the room were at the ages of the greatest variability. At least half of the girls in the room...had begun the first stages of adolescent puberty, while the other half had not begun at all."

Another observer echoes this with the added notice of developmental differences between the sexes: "...Some still looked like children, while others were quite tall and beginning to 'fill out.' The boys were generally behind the girls in development...."

The intellectual development options were probably most revealing and captivating to the participants, although with both the physical development and intellectual growth, instructional consequences were dramatically clear to these prospective teachers. For the intellectual development assignment, many participants completed the brief experiment in which a moral dilemma question is posed for the class and then each young adolescent answers. These responses are then analyzed at a later time against models on intellectual and moral development in order to experience a feeling for concrete and abstract thinking variation among middle schoolers.

Many ratios turned out similar to these results from two seventh grade classes: abstract thought = 1; transitional = 11; concrete thinking = 24 (The spread was roughly proportional in each class.). One observer summed it up: "You could see the concrete learners. They needed to know details; others could do it all."

Yet another describes a large group discussion with community speakers that he experienced: "The Halloween 'vandalism' day for the seventh graders gave me insight into the students' listening and reading abilities.... I was impressed with the knowledge and intellectual curiosity many students displayed.... Several students asked thought-provoking, hypothetical questions, while others still had very simple ones."

Observers saw clearly the cognitive readiness of many middle graders and the teachers' varied instructional attempts to "push" (in Ted Sizer's positive sense) this development. One college student notes: "...the use of journals is one such lesson activity to allow the students to write down about anything and to try and sort things out...."

Debriefing the process

When daily observations are complete at the middle level, teachers bring closure in various ways: "After class, I thank the participant for attending and usually ask what he thought of the lessons and any suggestions or questions he might have." Another says: "I ask if he has any questions/comments about the class periods observed."

Still another involves the middle schoolers themselves: "...I allow the students time to ask our visitor questions and our visitor time to ask students questions."

When the two-week experience (10 periods of classroom contact) ends, Wabash participants report for a de-briefing session with the college supervisor on campus. In a typical 40-45 minute session with generally 5-7 students present in a small group setting, each person shares a brief description of his placement (teams, grade levels, and assignments selected), then describes the one major insight about young adolescents' physical and/or intellectual development he gained.

Sometimes this phase of questioning is phrased as "What surprised you most about these kids' developmental characteristics?" Conversation picks up quickly as responses open up various debates, comparisons of insights are made, and attempts to explain discrepancies in the group's experiences are thrashed out. Inevitably, the final questions ask them to speculate, as beginning teachers, about how a teacher might accommodate instructionally for these developmental truths. Often, students relate how teachers handled instruction, and many share ideas they have begun to imagine. The session concludes with a brief overview of the next phase, the high school observation.

The evaluation phase

Both the classroom teachers and the college supervisor evaluate formally each participant's involvement. An evaluation form is sent to the team leader for each observer/participant assigned to the team and this is returned to the college and becomes part of the participant's teacher education file. The college supervisor evaluates the overall experience (the three parts) using teacher responses and the student's completed reflective observation log.

While Wabash students continue in the program and may specialize in working with older adolescents, all, by this introductory experience, are afforded the important opportunity to gaze reflectively at the young adolescent's growth and development within an institutional context. For many participants, these glimpses of the growth process and of the unique organization of the middle school designed to accommodate the uniqueness of this age stay with them, creating a larger understanding of student diversity, change, and developmental reality, regardless of their later level of teaching.

References
George, P., & Lawrence, G. (1982). *Handbook for middle school teaching.* Glenview, IL: Scott Foresman.

Using the Shadow Study Observation Technique

Thomas S. Dickinson

Georgia Southern University, a comprehensive institution recently granted university status, provides a wide variety of programs in arts and sciences, education, and the professions. The array of teacher education programs offered by GSU includes undergraduate and graduate degree programs with majors in middle grades. As such, the University prepares teachers who meet state certification requirements embodied in Georgia's separate 4-8 middle grades certificates.

Field experiences are an integral part of the GSU middle grades program. Upon completion of a mandated core of lower division liberal arts course work, students embark on a professional education sequence that integrates academic content in selected subject areas, professional education courses, and field experiences in middle level schools.

Because of its location in a small college town in southeast Georgia, education students are afforded field experiences in small city and rural school settings with diverse, multicultural student populations. Student teaching is accomplished within a large geographical region of southeast Georgia or in the urban environs of Atlanta. Supervision of all field experiences is provided by departmental teaching faculty or, in the case of student teaching in Atlanta, by full-time on-site university supervisors.

The middle grades program

The middle grades program is composed of five sequential quarters of coursework and a sixth quarter of student teaching. Each quarter contains a mixture of upper division content courses in two subject fields and middle grades professional education courses. All professional education courses in middle grades are block scheduled, team planned and taught, and contain a variety of field components.

Students begin with Cluster 1, **Introduction to Middle Grades Concept** which provides coursework in the characteristics of young adolescents, the rationale for a middle school, and middle school organization and curriculum. Field experiences move through structured observations in grades five through eight, to an all-day shadow study of an individual middle level student (the focus of this section), and include structured interviews with middle level students. Each of these experiences conclude with extended debriefings.

Clusters 2 through 4 follow similar patterns with students expanding the focus to include integration of curriculum, teaching skills and materials, strategies for flexible grouping, individual lesson and unit planning, and evaluation. Students in these clusters participate in a variety of classroom settings where they plan and teach interdisciplinary units as parts of teams.

Cluster 5 synthesizes the student's program in middle level education through a capstone field-based course that involves a 10-week practicum in the middle grades and which encompasses major responsibilities in interdisciplinary team planning and teaching, work with advisor-advisee sessions, and seminars to integrate and interpret these experiences. The final quarter of the program is a 10-week, full-time student teaching experience in a middle grades classroom.

Cluster 1, Introduction to Middle Grades Concept

Students in this initial cluster are concurrently enrolled in **MG 451, Introduction to the Middle Grades**, and **MG 452, Middle Grades Curriculum**. These two courses together focus on two foundations of middle level education—the nature and needs of young adolescents and developmentally appropriate schools. **MG 452, Middle Grades Curriculum**, has as its major field experience an all-day shadow study experience focusing on the young adolescent within the context of the school. Prior to their engagement in the shadow study observation, students have studied developmental aspects of early adolescence—physical, social, emotional, intellectual, and moral. Through extended simulations they have examined the organizational and curriculum components of middle level schools. As these foundations are laid in the classroom, students are prepared to integrate the world of practice into their development.

Preparations for the shadowing

Prior to the experience of actually shadowing a middle grades student, college students read *Life In The Three Sixth Grades* (Lounsbury & Johnston, 1988). Since the shadow experience parallels the national shadow studies that Lounsbury and others have conducted (Lounsbury & Clark, 1990; Lounsbury & Johnston, 1985; Lounsbury & Marani, 1964; Lounsbury, Marani, & Compton, 1980), this reading prepares students for both the observational technique and the analysis/synthesis of the observation. In addition, students begin to make linkages between early adolescent development and middle level schooling practices .

Students receive instruction in naturalistic observation techniques, unobtrusive observation, and note taking. Forms used in the observation are distributed and reviewed. These forms are modeled after those used in the national shadow studies. Finally, the ethical/confidentiality considerations of observation and reporting are explained and discussed.

Students are provided a packet of materials that outlines their responsibilities, provides checklists for both before and after the experience, observation/data collection forms, and a follow-up analysis/synthesis assignment. Each student is provided an individual student schedule, a school master schedule (in the case of a self-contained teacher, an individual teacher's schedule), and a building map. Students are excused from all classes for their shadow study day.

Depending upon the individual school's preference, students to be shadowed are identified by either the guidance counselor, the building principal, the first period teacher, or advisory teacher. Assignments have been arranged previously by the university instructor and building administrator or guidance counselor. All assignments (and potential replacements for absent students) are random except in the case of exceptionalities which entail extended resource room classes. Outside of this constraint, all students are eligible to be shadowed. To prevent overcrowding of a school by observers all placements are scheduled for only one observer per grade level per school per day. Shadow study experiences are also scheduled so that other field experiences are not ongoing in the school.

Each individual school site is prepared for this experience by a formal inservice program provided by university instructors which outlines the responsibilities of students and the background preparations for the experience that students have received. This session also delineates guidelines and expectations for teachers and the school community. Since most of the school sites which are used for the shadow study experience also serve as sites for other field work, it is a common occurrence for teachers and students to encounter university students in the buildings.

The shadow experience itself

On the day of the shadow experience students arrive 10-15 minutes before school starts, in professional attire, and with necessary materials in hand, including lunches. They check into the building according to individual school procedure and find the first period/initial classroom. Here the student to be shadowed is appropriately identified in an unobtrusive manner by the designated staff member. Students take a seat where they can observe the student and begin the day-long acquisition of information.

The process moves forward in a fixed sequence. Every five to seven minutes the exact time is recorded, followed by a brief narrative description of the specific student behavior at that time. Additionally, students record information about environmental factors (both physical and psychological) and keep a running commentary of their own comments or general impressions. As the day progresses, this sequence repeats itself again and again. Instructions to observers are framed thusly:

> While taking your samples and writing them down, continue to fade into the background. Since you are taking a snapshot every five to seven minutes you can briefly look at the student when the sample is to be taken, begin to record data, scan the room looking for environmental factors or continue to record your comments and impressions, observe other students, and then return for another snapshot.

Students are counseled to be in tune to a variety of student behaviors—entrance and exit modes, seat selection, hall behaviors, and peer relationships. A new time interval begins with each change of class, period, or subject. Students are instructed to use the "window" between data entries to provide a degree of flexibility in writing their observations and elaborating their comments. This provides the student the opportunity to use direct quotes and to begin to wonder about aspects of development, school structure, or instruction. As a result of ethical/confidentiality discussions students refer to their shadow study by a fictitious name in their data collection, or as simply "the student."

The observer's day is a continual repetition of beginnings, data collection, change of class. Students are relieved of their strict data collection responsibilities at lunch, but most continue to observe and record impressions later. Unlike the national shadow studies that include an interview with the shadow student at day's end, this application ends without an interview. Students return directly to the university and complete a narrative form that asks for their immediate impressions, reactions, and conclusions while the experience is still fresh in their minds.

Evaluations and reactions

University student reactions, especially those generated at the conclusion of the experience, are particularly insightful. One older student commented: "Today was absolutely exhausting! I will definitely be more sympathetic and understanding when my middle grades daughter complains about a 'rough day.' This experience will stay with me always; my future students will benefit from my experience—I can think of no better way for someone to really understand a student's day and appreciate their efforts."

The reality of the length of the day and the cycle of change that students go through consistently draws comment: "Although my immediate reactions were a bit delayed because of the drive back, I still distinctly remember how I felt as the last bell rang—exhausted! By the last period I was fidgeting as much as they were. I was very impressed at how well the students behaved, having to sit so long for so many long hours. It makes me wonder how I ever made it through middle school." Another student wrote: "These kids have a tough schedule! They have a 10 minute break in the morning, 30 minutes for lunch, and 10 minutes free in the afternoon. The rest of the time is spent in the classroom on task."

Having studied early adolescent development, the shadow study allows observers the opportunity to see aspects of development in action: "I could definitely see a wide range of physical and mental maturity. It was strange to see some of these kids almost as developed as myself while others were still so small. I realized how important the function of differentiation plays in a teacher's duty. A teacher must adapt to these individual needs and differences."

Teachers comment that as a result of the experience: "University students demonstrate a new-found respect for school—both what teachers and students go through on a day-in, day-out basis. It's interesting to see the 'realities' of the profession begin to dawn on them."

Another teacher offered: "I like having them around, especially since I don't have any idea who they're watching. I think it helps keep me on my toes. And their obvious enthusiasm is refreshing—for me and the kids."

Commenting on confidentiality, one administrator related: "My counselor identifies the students for the observers. While I know that, I still asked one young man 'Who are you shadowing?' His response, 'A student.' I appreciate the training these kids have had, even if I don't remember it always!"

Report of the study

Following the completion of the shadow study observation, students type their original notes onto fresh forms for readability. Using their collected data they then compose a major paper that summarizes and analyzes the experience. Students are reminded that their focus must be on the student and his or her day.

Students read and analyze their raw data to discover the best organizational construct. They have organized their paper using a chronological narrative, core *vs* non-core classes, student interests, continuing themes throughout a middle schooler's day, and the developmental characteristics of the student and the degree of fit (or non-fit) with the day.

Students compose their papers with an eye to their emerging knowledge of early adolescence and middle school curriculum and organization. While students can make commentary and analysis they are reminded to avoid judgements.

Individuals are debriefed following their observation in two ways. First, as students rotate back to class following their shadow study experience they share commentary with the class, focusing on revealing aspects that bring the reality of their class study to life. Secondly, students are debriefed individually in relation to their analysis paper prior to its composition. This debriefing helps students shape the final product.

Like all data collection techniques, the shadow study has its limitations, but the technique provides an intense look at a middle school student and also at the individual observer. It is a valid observation technique that enables students preparing to teach at the middle level to relate classroom understanding with real life.

References

Lounsbury, J.H., & Clark, D.C. (1990). *Inside grade eight: From apathy to excitement.* Reston, VA: National Association of Secondary School Principals.

Lounsbury, J. H., & Johnston, J. H. (1985). *How fares the ninth grade?* Reston, VA: National Association of Secondary School Principals.

Lounsbury, J. H., & Johnston, J. H. (1988). *Life in the three sixth grades.* Reston, VA: National Association of Secondary School Principals.

Lounsbury, J. H., & Marani, J. (1964). *The junior high school we saw: One day in the eighth grade.* Alexandria, VA: Association of Supervision and Curriculum Development.

Lounsbury, J. H., Marani, J. V., & Compton, M. F. (1980). *The middle school in profile: A day in the seventh grade.* Columbus, OH: National Middle School Association.

Interdisciplinary Intern Teaching Experience

C. Kenneth McEwin
J. Pat Knight

Appalachian State University is committed to the importance of field experiences and has designed a sequence of these opportunities for undergraduate Middle Grades Education majors. This section provides an overview of these experiences with a focus on the interdisciplinary internship.

Appalachian State University

Appalachian State University is a comprehensive university offering a broad range of undergraduate and graduate programs to 11,500 students. The Reich College of Education is an important part of the university and has a long history of teacher education. The College has the primary responsibility for the preparation of elementary, middle grades, secondary, and special subject teachers at the undergraduate and graduate levels. Degrees in school administration and other professional areas are also offered. Approximately 20 percent of all students at Appalachian are in one of the teacher preparation programs. The undergraduate and graduate Middle Grades Education degree programs are housed in the Department of Curriculum and Instruction. The programs have a coordinator with approximately 100 currently enrolled in the undergraduate program and 125 in the graduate program.

Middle grades education degrees

Appalachian State University established the first comprehensive middle grades teacher preparation program in North Carolina, and one of the first in the nation, in 1976. The program includes a strong focus on the study of young adolescents and their schools as well as an emphasis on strategies for successful teaching at the middle level. Double subject area concentrations are required at the undergraduate level with current choices including mathematics, science, language arts, and social studies.

The middle grades program began at ASU as a special track of the elementary education program. However, successful completion of the program now leads to a degree in Middle Grades Education. Middle grades certification is mandatory for teaching mathematics, science, language arts, and social studies in grades six through nine in North Carolina. The Middle Grades Education program is a separate degree program with its own identity and is treated as such. It has equal status with all other programs housed in the department and college.

The sophomore field experience

The first field experience for Middle Grades Education majors is **Curriculum and Instruction 2800, Introduction to Teaching**. This course is required of all teacher education majors. It is a four semester hour course designed as "the basic conceptual introduction to the world of public education and the teaching of regular and special needs students." In addition to four hours of classroom seminars per week, 45 hours of observation and participation are required.

Introduction to Teaching provides students with experiences that enable them to better understand the roles and responsibilities of teaching. It also provides opportunities for prospective teachers to acquire and develop insights and understandings into the interrelatedness of theory and practice. The world of teaching is openly evaluated with students being encouraged to express their thoughts regarding the profession and their careers in teaching.

The early field experiences included in this course also provide students with the opportunity to make more informed decisions about their choice of teaching as a career. A small number of students change career choices after the classroom experiences while others change grade levels or content areas. However, the large majority become excited about their chosen profession and greatly appreciate the opportunity to spend some structured time in public school classrooms early in their professional preparation.

The Interdisciplinary Internship

Curriculum and Instruction 3140, Interdisciplinary Internship is a three semester hour course/internship that is taken during the second junior semester or first senior semester. It is taken concurrently with five other accelerated classes during the "internship block." These courses are taught during the first 10 weeks of the 15 week semester. The seminar portion of the class meets 4 hours per week for 10 weeks with the remaining 5 weeks of the semester being spent serving an internship in a middle grades classroom (grades 6-9). Several other professional courses are also taken by the interns during the first 10 weeks. All classes taught during the 10 weeks meet for the same number of clock hours they would if they were taught during the usual 15 week semester. An example of the block plan is provided below:

10 Weeks of Class Meetings	5 Week Internship
Two two-hour methods courses/ subject area concentrations (4)	Five week internship Full day, every day
Reading in the Content Areas (2)	
The Middle Level School (3)	
Interdisciplinary Internship (3)	
Audiovisual Instruction (2)	

Scheduling the class meetings and internship seminars exclusively during the first 10 weeks allows students to spend the last five weeks of the semester in the school classroom. It provides interns with a continuous experience over an extended time period. It also allows them to experience the total instructional day as opposed to spending only a specified number of hours in the classroom on selected days of the week. This plan prevents internship experiences from being primarily random and based on individual students' class schedules rather than on other more professional considerations.

Professors teaching the classes in the internship state that students become more readily immersed in the content of the courses and that the experience assumes a more realistic flavor since students know they will very soon be teaching middle level students. The internship block also provides the professors teaching methods courses during the first 10 weeks the opportunity to follow up on what they have taught as it may be utilized in middle level classrooms. Instructors also have the option of making assignments to be completed during the internship since grades for block courses are not given until the end of the semester.

Interdisciplinary Internship goals and objectives

The course/internship is based on a number of goals and objectives including providing prospective middle level teachers with: (a) an intensive in-classroom experience teaching young adolescents, (b) the opportunity of working with student colleagues in developing interdisciplinary units and teaching those units as a member of an interdisciplinary team, (c) practical experience in linking theory and practice, (d) the experience of working with and learning from practicing middle level teachers, (e) opportunities to become knowledgeable about teaching materials including state adopted textbooks, (f) opportunities to work with special needs students, and (g) opportunities to use learning programs involving subjects taught in the middle grades.

Classroom teachers working with the interns are positive about the experience and frequently state their support for the program. One cooperating teacher recently stated that "the blocking arrangement definitely allows students to experience the real world of teaching. The interns have the opportunity to apply what they have learned on campus in the reality of a middle level classroom setting."

Placement and roles of interns

The Director of Field Experiences, in cooperation with the interdisciplinary internship course instructor, places several interns in each school. Principals play an active role in these placements and classroom teachers work with interns on a volunteer basis. Placements are made based on factors such as the academic preparations of students and the availability of competent, experienced teachers. Care is also taken that students from several disciplines are assigned to the same school so that interdisciplinary units can be planned and taught during the internship experience.

The Director of Field Experiences made the following comments on the placement process: "Initially a potential problem in locating placements that were compatible with the goals and objectives of the interdisciplinary internship was envisioned. However, that problem did not occur. It is now a common occurrence for cooperating teachers to request two interns. The resulting multiple placements have provided even more opportunities for interns to work together as members of interdisciplinary teams."

Interns spend the majority of their time working with cooperating teachers and assisting with instruction in their subject areas. However, a major goal of the internship is the provision of opportunities to teach interdisciplinary units with fellow intern colleagues from different subject areas. It would be desirable to place all interns in middle level schools that incorporate interdisciplinary units into the curriculum on a regular basis. This is not always possible. However, including the requirement of teaching two such units during the internship assures that all middle grades majors will have some experience planning and teaching with teachers from disciplines other than their own.

Interns have already completed **Introduction to Teaching** and the majority of their other professional courses when they arrive at the schools to begin their internships. Therefore, they are ready to spend time observing, getting to know students, and assuming teacher-assistant type duties. The length of time spent in this observation/learning period varies according to the abilities and previous experience of the individuals involved.

They assume responsibilities for small group instruction and begin preparation for teaching interdisciplinary units with one or more of their student intern colleagues as they become more comfortable with the teaching environment and gain self confidence through experience. Planning sessions are held in the schools with all parties concerned having input into the teaching of these units. Interns are complimentary of the experiences gained during the internship. They often make both written and oral statements such as: "The internship experience I just completed was one of the most important parts of my preparation to become a teacher. I was able to go right into the classroom and immediately become involved in working with seventh grade students and their teachers."

The interdisciplinary units

The instructor of the interdisciplinary class, **CI 3140, Interdisciplinary Internship**, is also responsible for supervision of the interns with each student being visited a minimum of one time per week during the five-week period. An additional responsibility of the instructor is that of contacting cooperating teachers early in each semester to obtain topics for the interdisciplinary units. This allows interns who will be working together in the same school to develop interdisciplinary units on topics selected by the cooperating teachers before the internship begins. In many instances, interns will meet with their cooperating teachers to obtain input as they begin to develop these units. The design of these units is completed during the first 10 weeks of class time with the guidance and assistance of the university instructor.

Interns are typically very interested in developing these units since they are aware they will be teaching them to middle grades students at a later time. Cooperating teachers are pleased since the students present rather comprehensive and elaborate units that address topics which are a part of the planned curriculum. Cooperating teachers often ask to retain the units for future use. A typical comment from a student evaluating the internship is: "Working with other interns to plan an interdisciplinary unit you know you will be teaching in a few weeks is a rewarding experience. It gave me the opportunity to meet and plan with my cooperating teacher before the internship actually began. I even got to meet the kids I would be teaching. This was exciting and gave me confidence." Interns also frequently point out the importance of working with other interns with different academic concentrations in designing and implementing the units.

Courses taken during the internship block

As previously noted, several other courses are taken during the first 10 weeks of the block semester. **Curriculum and Instruction 4150, The Middle Level School** is a three-hour course which covers many middle level topics such as "the young adolescent" and the "middle school concept." It is a "programmatic study of the components of effective middle level schools based on the developmental characteristics of early adolescents and middle grades research. The course investigates the middle school philosophy and focuses on selected aspects such as the interdisciplinary team organization, exploratory curricula, and teacher-based guidance programs." **Reading in the Content Areas** and **Audiovisual Instruction** are other courses included in the block semester.

Students also take the two methods courses that correspond with the two subject area concentrations they have selected. These methods courses are designed specifically for middle grades majors. Middle grades majors are not placed in classes designed for teachers of young children or senior high school youth. It is considered essential that special courses be offered that address directly and exclusively the knowledge and skills needed by middle level teachers. Sample course titles are **Teaching Social Studies in the Middle Grades** and **Teaching Science in the Middle Grades**.

All methods courses are two semester hours. Students greatly appreciate the opportunity to take courses where instructors can focus directly and exclusively on the middle level. They also support the plan to place these methods courses in the block schedule format. As one student noted, "taking methods courses in the block allows you to utilize the information learned directly and almost immediately. You even realize that theory and practice are not so far apart after all."

Evaluation of interdisciplinary internship block

The courses, internship, and related experiences that make up the block semester are evaluated in a number of ways. Students complete an extensive formal evaluation of each instructor and course. Individual instructors and supervisors use a variety of other instruments to receive feedback. Evaluation is also an important topic considered at monthly planning meetings attended by instructors and supervisors who teach in the program.

Additionally, the departmental chairperson meets with students at the conclusion of their internship and again near the end of student teaching to obtain feedback regarding the internship semester. Suggestions for improvements are openly solicited during these meetings. A formal written evaluation of all courses involved in the internship block is obtained near the end of the student teaching semester with results being forwarded to departmental chairpersons and instructors. Informal evaluative input is also obtained through conversations among teachers, principals, the Director of Field Experiences, and university instructors.

Student evaluation

The traditional letter grading system is used in all block courses including the **Interdisciplinary Internship**. Grades for the classes completed during the first 10 weeks are not issued until the end of the semester. Therefore, instructors may elect to give assignments to be completed during the internship portion of the semester. Methods instructors, in some instances, elect to observe students during their internship. This tends to occur most frequently when specific students need individual assistance. The overall supervision of interns, however, remains the responsibility of the **Interdisciplinary Internship** instructor.

The **Interdisciplinary Internship** instructor/supervisor meets with the cooperating public school teachers and the interns at the end of the internship for evaluation purposes. This practice provides the cooperating teacher with input into the final evaluation and grade assigned to the interns. Students must receive a grade of "C" or higher in all block courses and the internship to enter student teaching the following semester.

Concluding remarks

This section provided a brief look at one institution's plan and offered the reader the opportunity to consider some alternatives to traditional field experience models. Teacher preparation institutions, in cooperation with school districts and state departments of education, should boldly move ahead by establishing and maintaining strong preparation programs designed specifically for middle level education. Certainly, carefully planned, comprehensive field experiences with young adolescents are a vital part of this preparation.

Pre-Student Teaching Immersion

Larry M. Putbrese

Program background

In many states, certification regulations exist to guide preparation and provide a basis for licensing teachers. In Minnesota, elementary education majors are licensed to teach grades one through six. Secondary education majors are licensed for a particular major(s) or minor(s) in grades seven through twelve.

In 1976, teachers in Minnesota middle schools responded to a questionnaire regarding the discrepancies between actual teaching expectations and undergraduate teacher preparation programs. The results of this survey ultimately led to the Board of Teaching Rule 5 MCAR 3.054, Teachers in Middle Schools. This Rule requires people seeking a middle school endorsement on their original license to participate in a program containing a minimum of twenty-four quarter hours credit.

The Board of Teaching prescribes certain required components in the approved program. Clearly, this Rule supports the propositions that young adolescents: (a) are unique, when compared to elementary or secondary students; (b) need to be taught differently from students in other levels; (c) need a developmentally appropriate program which responds to the physical, intellectual, social, and emotional needs of individuals within the collective group; and (d) deserve to be taught by teachers who are specially prepared to focus upon the unique learning needs of these pupils. In the fall of 1984, St. Cloud State University responded to this opportunity by creating the **Early Adolescent Block Program** for undergraduate students.

Organizational structure

The **Early Adolescent Block Program** aids students in determining their suitability for middle level teaching and prepares them for effective teaching at this level. Successful completion of the Block experience adds a middle school endorsement to the licensure of participating elementary and secondary education students.

The Block consists of 19 quarter credits of course offerings, reflecting the components required by the Board of Teaching Rule. These components include philosophy and organization of the middle school, interdisciplinary teaming, psychology, and special learning disabilities. This content is conveyed by integrating university seminars with an immersion field experience in a middle school. The three Block components include: a three week intensive on-campus seminar, seven to eight weeks of full time participation in schools, and weekly on-site seminars that integrate theory and practice during the field experience.

In addition to the 19 credit Block, the Rule requires elementary education majors to fulfill a twelve credit subject concentration (minimum) in each curricular area in which licensure is desired. The Rule requires secondary education majors to complete developmental and remedial reading components as well as the Block.

Demographic profile of participants

Students entering the Block must be admitted to teacher education. Because their cooperating teachers hold high expectations of them in terms of being prepared to write lesson plans and conduct lessons, most students postpone registering for the Block until the quarter before student teaching.

Participation in the **Early Adolescent Block** is optional for teacher education students. Approximately 5-8% of the teacher education candidates at St. Cloud State University select this option. Since the program's inception in 1984, it continues to attract more students. Only twelve students participated in the program in 1984-85 compared to more than forty students during 1990-91. Approximately two thirds of the program participants are elementary education majors.

Field experience placement procedures

Two middle level schools serve as placement sites for all Block students. One contains grades five through seven with the other housing grades seven and eight. Students receive two different placements during the field experience. Each segment is approximately four weeks and both are in the same building.

A student's certification level affects placement. Elementary education majors are required to have a teaching experience component with 7th, 8th, or 9th graders. They receive this in at least one of the two field assignment segments, plus experience in the subject concentration in which they will receive licensure. Secondary education majors receive at least one of the four week field experiences with 5th or 6th graders in their area of subject matter concentration.

The second field experience segment is in an academic area other than the licensure area. It is felt that, by doing this, the university is making a statement countering the perpetuation of "subject matter specialization" so typical of secondary education programs. This act "forces" university students to visualize the young adolescent and the middle level program as more of a "whole," rather than through the eyes of a subject matter specialist. Although the student may request particular curricular areas, most assignments, after attending to the requirements of the Rule, are made randomly. All field placements are made through collaborative consultation between the university coordinator, the building principal and interested teachers.

Preparation for the field experience

The **Early Adolescent Block** is offered during the Fall and Winter quarters each year. Continued growth is likely to necessitate adding a Block during Spring Quarter as well. During the first three weeks of the quarter, students attend on-campus seminars with university instructors from 9:00 a.m. until 4:00 p.m. A team of three faculty, representing teacher development, early adolescent education, and special education, cooperatively plan the seminar. The content is presented topically rather than being divided into discrete courses. Discussion revolves around early adolescence, teachers, schools, and programs. It serves as an orientation to early adolescent education and sets the stage for the field experience component.

While in seminars, Block students progressively learn the complexities of middle level education, including a great deal of information about such activities as interdisciplinary teaming, advisor/advisee programs, learning styles, cooperative learning, learning centers, and the intellectual, physical, emotional, and social development of early adolescents. Students develop interdisciplinary units, learning centers, and affective education activities which they will apply during the field experience component. Thus, the seminar provides the theoretical and practical foundations necessary to help assure a successful field experience.

Field experience seminar/professional activities

A one and one-half hour period of time is reserved each week of the field experience component for a seminar. These sessions are taught by university faculty and representatives from the placement site middle schools. The principal, curriculum coordinator, and classroom teachers all share their expertise at the seminars. Topics explored stem from a core of professional knowledge and concerns/issues that emerge during the course of the field experience including essential elements of instruction, outcome-based education, curriculum development procedures, and the like. Further collaboration takes place when the university coordinator teaches at the middle level schools in order to enable teachers to participate in the seminars.

During these seminars, discussion focuses on what students have learned, observed, questioned and challenged during the field experience. They reflect on each week's activities and, as a result, make some astonishing self-discoveries. They often reveal that they are learning things and did not realize they were learning them!

A former Block student comments on one such discovery: "My biggest concern going into the field experience was 'Eeek! Some of these kids are bigger than I am! Am I going to be able to teach them and discipline them as effectively as I do elementary students?' After the first day, I realized that dealing with students this age wasn't necessarily more difficult than dealing with elementary students, it was just different! After that, I relaxed and just enjoyed working with them."

During the seminar, assignments for specific observations and activities are made for the next week of the field experience. In this way, theory and on-the-job training are interwoven resulting in relevant experiences for students. A student describes this integration of theory and practice following a discussion of mainstreaming: "One of our requirements for the block was to choose a student who was currently on an IEP, observe that student, recording what happened in class, and observing how effective the plan was for that particular student."

In addition to the seminars, **Early Adolescent Block** students further develop their professional knowledge base and identities by attending national and regional middle school conferences. Although distance and financial considerations result in infrequent participation at the National Middle School Association's Annual Conference, students regularly attend the Midwest Regional Middle Level Educators Conference. **Early Adolescent Block** students receive free registration in return for assisting at the conference. They are amazed at the activities associated with the conference and the quality of the presentations. Furthermore, the conference offers students the opportunity to network with other pre-service professionals interested in middle level education. Several Block students reflect on the benefits of attending conferences.

"I really enjoyed attending the Regional Conference last fall. I found it to be a great source of information, and was happy to be able to meet so many other middle level educators and administrators."

"The regional conference provided several benefits. It gave us the opportunity to attend sessions on topics that interested each of us, personally.

We were able to make contact with other middle school instructors and share questions and concerns. Making the trip also gave our Block time to be together and promote team unity."

Role of the principal

The principals of the two middle level schools serving as the field experience sites play multiple roles in assuring the effectiveness of this program. They are actively involved in the Block program during the planning, implementation, and evaluation phases. Each quarter, the principals confer with the **Early Adolescent Block** Coordinator to schedule the program. Next, they identify the faculty members who will serve as cooperating teachers and assist with placement assignments.

Upon the arrival of the university students on visitation day immediately prior to the field experience, the principals give an orientation to their schools covering school philosophy, curriculum, activities and policies. In addition, cooperating teachers receive information regarding the university students' backgrounds, preparation, and interests. During the field experience, principals informally observe students and conduct some of the seminar sessions. Upon completion of the field experience, principals and staff members evaluate the overall effectiveness of the program and share this input with the Block Coordinator.

As a result of their direct involvement in the Block Program, the principals strongly support it. They feel that the presence of these students often rekindles enthusiasm and strengthens faculty commitment to middle level education.

Role of the cooperating teacher

When students first arrive at their middle level school, teachers provide an orientation to their classrooms and programs. One teacher's comments illustrate the focus of the orientation: "I sit down and find out their previous experiences and discuss their expectations. We also go over classroom rules, school rules, etc....and discuss my expectations of them. By setting some clear goals and by easing them into the classroom situation at a pace they are comfortable with we can assure a positive experience." Based on this interaction, teachers and students collaboratively plan the scope of the field experience.

Cooperating teachers aid university students in understanding the instructional implications of early adolescents' developmental characteristics. Students get to see teachers model appropriate middle school instructional strategies and then practice such strategies themselves.

Throughout the experience, cooperating teachers provide feedback to students. "Communication is a key to a successful experience. We discuss the daily experience and evaluate in a positive manner," states one teacher.

While a Block student teaches, cooperating teachers play multiple roles as expressed by a math teacher: "I would be a combination spectator, observer, ally, mentor, and evaluator.... I would evaluate the Block student on the qualities required for successful teaching: competency in subject, communication skills, inspiring values and personality traits, understanding and acceptance of students, and competency in professional knowledge."

At the end of each segment of the field experience, in addition to daily comments, the student receives a written evaluation from the cooperating teacher describing strengths as well as pointing out areas which need improvement. The open-ended evaluation form asks them to list specific activities the student engaged in and to describe their impressions of the student as an effective middle level teacher. This feedback, as well as the experience itself, assists future teachers in deciding if they are best suited for middle level teaching.

Role of the university student

During the field experience component, university students fulfill the same hours as the teachers of the assigned school. This provides them with ample time to meet with their teachers to plan for and evaluate their classroom participation experiences.

Comments from cooperating teachers highlight their goals for students. "One of the main goals of the program is to have students 'test the waters' with middle level students to see if the middle school is where the future teachers would like to work." "The philosophy of a middle school setting is unique and different from other school settings and this experience allows students to 'experience' and 'live' this philosophy." A Block student adds: "The main goal of the field experience was to provide us with hands-on experience in dealing with students at an exciting/confusing time of their lives." These goals guide and direct students' experiences.

While at the schools, university students assume the multiple roles of effective middle level teachers. They address the affective developmental needs of students by serving as co-advisors for an advisory group throughout the entire field experience. This gives them the opportunity to use activities developed during the seminar. As a result of this role, university students and young adolescents find bonds developing that are not easily forgotten upon completion of their Block experience.

Since teachers at both participating schools are organized into interdisciplinary teams, students also develop their teaming skills. Many have the opportunity to teach interdisciplinary units prepared during the seminar.

During the field experience, students assume increasing responsibility ranging from "housekeeping" tasks to teaching the entire class. One cooperating teacher explains a typical progression into the program: "The student generally begins with observation, correcting papers, and assisting individuals and small groups. Gradually the student broadens out to working with large groups." A Block student elaborates on this process further: "I began my experience as an observer and gradually took on more responsibilities such as running the advisor/advisee program in my home room, teaching classes outside of my major field, developing a learning center and performing many of the duties of a teacher of early adolescents."

The seminar preparation makes students eager to "try out" their knowledge. Upon arrival at their placement site, they immediately become immersed in the teacher's daily routine. Some of the other experiences gained by students include: (a) small and large group presentations; (b) evaluating student performance; (c) running errands and completing tasks for their cooperating teacher, such as making copies of worksheets, bulletin board displays, and the like; (d) developing transparencies for presentations; (e) assisting students with make-up work following absences; (f) working with and supervising students in a variety of settings; (g) participating in inservice activities; and (h) participating in parent-teacher conferences.

Role of the university supervisor

Three faculty members serve as university supervisors during the field experience. They spend a total of two days per week at each school. During this time, the supervisors seek feedback from the cooperating teachers, observe students periodically, and assure that the students participate in a broad range of appropriate middle school experiences. They encourage cooperating teachers to provide many teaching opportunities for students. Throughout the field experience, supervisors give students evaluative feedback. Thus, university supervisors wear many hats—they offer support and encouragement to students, monitor the quality of the field experiences, collaborate with cooperating teachers in providing feedback and structuring the field component, and assure that the program prepares students to be effective middle level teachers.

Enhancing professional development

Early Adolescent Block participants receive hundreds of hours of intense, but informative contact with young adolescents during the field experience. The feedback they receive from these students and cooperating teachers, plus the activities they experience, cause Block students to gain a great deal of confidence in their individual qualities and abilities. Their decision to enter the teaching profession is confirmed and they eagerly look forward to student teaching and, eventually, to having their own classrooms.

Teaching at the middle level is not for everyone. The field experience enables participants to make appropriate decisions regarding whether or not they decide to become a middle school teacher. Occasionally, students not demonstrating a high level of competency or interest in working with early adolescents are advised that they will not be recommended for this licensure.

The **Early Adolescent Block** meets its objectives. For the first time in Minnesota history, hiring officials can employ teachers for middle level teaching with specific age-appropriate training. It is rewarding to listen to administrators describe how well former Block students they hired are doing. They report that these persons are, although they may not realize it, functioning as "change agents" in that school. These school officials express pleasure at no longer having to make a choice between a secondary or an elementary person and hope for the best.

Students completing the Block Program note its benefits as evidenced by the following two statements.

"My experiences in the **Early Adolescent Block** were great! I had the opportunity to work with two very different teachers and saw how they dealt with young adolescents. I greatly appreciate the time I was able to spend with the students—both one on one and in large groups. The block was ideal in preparing me for the position I currently hold: that of a middle school English instructor."

"The **Early Adolescent Block** was the most helpful, positive experience I have had in my educational training. I liked the combination being on campus and working in the field. I found the information on the total student extremely important and helpful. In most programs you either learn what you're supposed to teach or some methods of presenting material, but you never get into the most important part, the student."

Additional contributors to this report include the following teachers: Jim Johnson, Donald A. Quickstad, and Jan Sorenson; and students: Kari A. Laine, Kem Preimesberger, and Toni Zinsli.

Part III

Models of Student Teaching at the Middle Level

A Multiple Site Model

Edward N. Brazee
John W. Pickering

Establishing student teaching experiences in the middle grades is a complicated endeavor influenced by the lack of specific middle level certification or the existence of overlapping elementary and secondary certificates. In addition, student teaching programs must also deal with such related middle grades issues as the grade and school configuration that house young adolescent students. The University of Maine, through a unique combination of university and school resources, has developed a student teaching program in the middle grades that deals with these and other concerns.

Context of the middle level student teaching experience

Upon entering the College of Education as a freshman or first semester sophomore, the student is assigned to a Professional Preparation Team (PPT). This team, one of sixteen located in school districts within a forty mile radius of the University of Maine, consists of a teacher educator from the College of Education, a graduate student, four to six teachers representing their respective schools, and approximately twenty-five students.

Student membership on the team usually includes eight or nine freshmen, seven sophomores, and the rest juniors and seniors. The educator members of the PPT are responsible for designing, conducting, and evaluating the students' experiences every time they are in the schools. These experiences are coordinated with the professional coursework students receive in the College of Education.

In their first two years students spend approximately 160 hours in their school district. In the junior year students combine their methods courses with experiences in the schools, arriving at their senior PPT internship (student teaching) with well over 200 hours of experience in classrooms.

Student teaching consists of two eight week experiences; the first in their own PPT and the second in their own PPT, another local PPT, a school district elsewhere in Maine, or in a sponsored program in Canada or England. In their first placement they work with a cooperating teacher with whom they have already spent considerable time. Their first experiences in the classroom include planning, teaching, and evaluating lessons, working with small groups of students, monitoring the playground, and assisting in parent conferences. Near the end of their eight weeks they assume full responsibility for class instruction.

Most student teachers arrange their second placement before starting their first assignment. Their teacher educator assists them in selecting a placement that expands their experience to another grade level, school, or in some cases, another country. Both the teacher educator and members of the PPT pay particular attention to selecting placements which will strengthen those areas of student performance still needing attention.

Although Maine is considering middle level certification, the current overlapping K-8 or 7-12 certification means that students have to select either an elementary or secondary option. The option for two student teaching experiences is then especially important for anyone contemplating teaching at the middle level because it allows prospective teachers to "sample" the middle level while still fulfilling student teaching in their level of certification, elementary or secondary.

University clinical supervision of the students during their first eight weeks is provided by the teacher educator. Then, depending on whether the student is located nearby or at a distance during the second placement, university clinical supervision is provided by the teacher educator or another supervisor designated by the College of Education.

Preparation for student teaching

During the semester prior to student teaching, students are enrolled in a **Senior Seminar** which meets for several hours biweekly and focuses on such issues as classroom management, certification, professional behavior, and other topics selected by students.

During the semester students participate in their methods course field experience in the classroom of the cooperating teacher with whom they will student teach. The field experience consists of planning, teaching, and evaluating lessons, working with small groups of students, and observing teaching styles, classroom management approaches, and student interactions. The student thus has the chance to get to know both the behaviors typical of students in that classroom, as well as becoming familiar with the approach of the teacher.

Demographic profile of student teachers

Approximately twenty-four PPT students student teach in middle level schools each year. Two-thirds of them are female. Most students in PPT are traditional students coming directly to college from high school. However, several are older non-traditional students. About 90% come from Maine, with the remainder coming from other New England states.

The PPT program comprises half of all the student teaching placements made each year. A larger portion of students not on PPT teams are non-traditional students who are older. These students do not have the extensive and early involvement with one school as do PPT students.

Placement procedures

Standards for student teaching require that students finish all required coursework, achieve an overall grade point average of 2.5, and have the recommendation of their college advisor and PPT. At the end of each year in PPT, students receive a summative evaluation from their supervisors, as well as a recommendation that they continue in education. By the time they have reached their student teaching experience, considerable evaluation of their abilities has taken place.

Initially, students are placed randomly in PPT sites. During the three and one half years in the schools they have opportunities to work with many teachers. Often there will be a mutual liking which develops between several teachers and a student. By the time to select a placement for the student teaching internship, the student has several teachers with whom to work. The student makes a request to the PPT and the team. In cooperation with the teacher selected, the building principal and the College of Education Coordinator of Educational Field Experiences make the final assignment.

Initial contacts

Due to the nature of the PPT structure, students have considerable experience with the teacher and students prior to student teaching. Similarly, because the teacher educator is in the schools of only one school district, that person is very well known by teachers and administrators in the district. PPT Building Representatives insure that students get introduced to the teachers with whom they will work. Their role becomes less vital each year the student is in the school since students become familiar with the school, faculty, and students.

What student teachers say about student teaching

The student teacher's first placement is always within the PPT site. The second student teaching placement may be within the PPT site or outside. In either case, student teachers indicated that they did have input into placement procedures. "For me, my input was adequate; I feel I had a voice in where I should be placed." A second student responded, "At first we were just placed in different schools; later we could ask for a grade level or subject and at the end we could be specific about what we wanted, although we could not get what we wanted sometimes."

The student teaching experience

The student teaching experience appears to be a powerful force in shaping attitudes and skills about teaching. It is during this time that students have opportunities to try out techniques and methods, to test their beliefs, and to begin to establish what will someday be their own style of teaching. After student teaching, one student wrote: "I found total classroom control/take-over the most helpful. I was able to go on field trips and attend conferences. The whole student teaching experience was very valuable. I enjoyed discussions with other teachers."

Another student spoke about the increased confidence which the internship provided: "My student teaching experiences were crucial in providing me with the confidence to assume my own classroom. It is hard because it's not real sometimes but being in the stream of things is crucial." And still another student referred to the practical: "The program gave us hands-on experience which in my opinion is the best. We got to see other styles of teaching."

Students want to be actively involved in student teaching. They do not want to sit passively by; in fact, they want to be actively involved from the beginning. In speaking about responsibilities during student teaching and the subsequent evaluation of those activities, one student teacher noted: "In the junior high school I was responsible for all classes, including study halls and work conference periods. I also interacted with parents of my students. My high school experience handed over responsibility more slowly, but at an adequate rate for more complex teaching preparation and students. I always had input in my evaluations."

Another student teacher said: "Responsibilities and expectations were to act professionally in all matters, gradually taking over total classroom control. My final evaluation was written by myself and cooperating teachers during conferences with a final grade agreed on by all parties."

A third student teacher, perhaps experiencing the paperwork of teaching for the first time, said: "There were always forms to fill out! Usually the forms were on our experiences. At the end of each semester we would have interviews to discuss our grade and fill out self-evaluation forms."

The responsibilities and expectations for student teaching vary with individual teachers in different placements. Generally, however, student teachers are expected to take on the roles and responsibilities of teachers in planning and organizing lessons, evaluating students and themselves, meeting with parents, attending meetings and participating in all functions of the school. These expectations appear to be common across all schools.

Importance of multiple sites for student teaching

Students who taught at two different sites were very specific in extolling the values of multiple site student teaching. One student said: "You can see the differences in ages, sizes, school politics, parents, curriculum, and maturity (or lack of it), etc."

Student teachers had opportunities to work with different grade levels. This was a valuable way to learn about characteristics of different age levels. "Because I car-pooled with other teachers I learned a lot more backdoor information which was very interesting and helpful. I had the experience of teaching 5th grade for 8 weeks, then 8th grade for 8 weeks. The contrast was tremendous. I learned the many differences of 8th and 5th graders and that I would enjoy teaching either grade."

Given the current lack of a middle-level teaching certificate in Maine and with overlapping K-8 elementary certification or 7-12 secondary certification, student teaching at two different sites seems especially important. "I feel that the double experience is absolutely necessary for someone in my position where I'll be certified for middle level and high school (7-12). The experiences were radically different and each had points which made me appreciate the other."

Whether multiple site student teaching permits a student to gain experience at two different levels (i.e. middle level and high school) or whether it allows for a wider range of experiences at the middle level, it appears that the multiple site model has not been fully utilized. The possibilities for this model are many in introducing prospective teachers to different developmental levels, organizations, and curricula.

Student teacher involvement with school personnel

Although student teachers have much early involvement in their PPT schools, the PPT Building Representatives vary in the intensity of their involvement. In one school the representative indicates that she is involved in the following manner: "I do give each student teacher a handbook, map, rules, regulations, rankbook, planbook, and other pertinent information. The cooperating teacher usually does the introductions to administration and faculty the student has not previously met." At another school the Building Representative sees it as his responsibility to "remain as a resource for all student teachers."

Schools where student teachers are placed range in size from less than one hundred students to the four hundred twenty-five students described by this Building Representative: "We are a mill community where most of the parents are employed. We do have a fair amount of low-income housing developments which does increase the incoming-outgoing school population throughout the year."

Another Building Representative characterizes her school in this manner: "Our middle school composition is grades 6-8 and houses 155 students. We have intramural, interscholastic, and enrichment programs that supplement our solid, core curriculum. There is a strong community commitment and support for the school."

Since there are fifteen different PPT sites, students have a wide diversity in experiences in their own school district. Having the opportunity to move to another site after the first eight week placement gives the student an opportunity to experience a different approach to educating students from diverse backgrounds.

Teacher expectations of the student teacher

Teachers expect that student teachers will bring many qualities to the experiences in the classroom. One teacher describes the following qualities: "Professionalism and responsibility are the most important qualities to me. The student teacher must conduct herself in a professional manner in relationships with students and staff. She must accept the responsibility for her daily preparations and long range planning. She must be a positive contributor to the educational process."

Another teacher was more specific regarding both expectations and requirements: "Expectations: to be well versed in basic math skills and Algebra I. Also the connection of these to higher level math courses and their applications. Requirements: to be present and willing to work hard! Also to be able to accept constructive criticism."

In addition to knowledge of subject and professional behavior another teacher indicated that there was a need for student teachers to "have a working knowledge of the age group."

Supervision and conferencing

There are many supervisory styles used throughout the PPT sites since each team decides how it will provide guidance and evaluation to the student teacher. One teacher describes her approach as follows: "I supervise each new teaching situation closely and assist in the development of lesson plans and unit development. Eventually my presence in the classroom becomes less frequent. I also offer opportunities to explore ideas and designs initiated by the student teacher."

Another says: "I don't use a special model. I closely supervise all facets in the beginning. As the student gains confidence, it becomes less structured. Eventually the student has full freedom of all aspects of the class."

Conferencing

Teachers report approximately the same approach to conferencing. They place much importance on frequent contact, as evidenced by the comments of this teacher: "We have daily conferences. In the morning we determine an overview of the forthcoming lessons. In the afternoon we conference to determine the strengths and weaknesses of the events, lessons, etc., of the day. The involvement is with the student teacher and myself. I have also asked the vice principal to evaluate at least one lesson."

Another teacher describes the conferencing procedure in this manner: "A great deal of informal conferencing takes place throughout the teaching experience. Several times a day the student meets with me. Other teachers and administrators observe the student and talk about their observations."

Evaluation process

Formative evaluations occur regularly during the student teacher's experience. Three or four times during student teaching the teacher educator, the cooperating teacher, and the student teacher meet to conduct a more formal summative evaluation. Each PPT conducts the conference differently. Of primary importance in all evaluations, however, is the interaction of the participants in determining together the areas still needing additional attention. Student teachers are encouraged to share their evaluations of progress made and those areas still needing work. At the end of each formal conference a written summary is completed by the cooperating teacher and by the teacher educator.

Enhancement of professional development

Teachers definitely gain from their involvement with student teachers. They list many benefits.

"I think it really helps me develop better lessons because it makes me think more about what ways of presentation are more effective."

"It allows you to look inward and do a great deal of evaluation of yourself and your teaching techniques. It also forces you to pay attention to many details which would ordinarily be overlooked."

"It is refreshing to see a different perspective concerning new techniques in education and to see my class in a different light. I like sharing ideas and using this person as a resource when dealing with classroom situations. My students benefit greatly."

What young adolescent students think about student teachers

Although it is often difficult to measure the impact of student teachers on the students they teach, student comments indicate that there are many positive results from the student teacher's involvement. One student wrote: "It is nice to have a variety. There is more time for the regular teacher to prepare and there is more individual help. It is nice to have younger ones with fresher minds."

Another young adolescent highlighted several different aspects of a student teacher's presence: "You are presented with two well thought out points of view. The material is sometimes new to the student teacher; therefore, they sometimes will form opinions about the literature as the class is forming theirs. It also allows us to observe someone as they grow in a profession."

Students seem to relate well to people they perceive to be still learning themselves. One stressed the value of seeing the student teacher as a learner: "They seem to relate to us better because they are still in school and need to work and suffer failed tests, bad homework, and late work."

One student wrote eloquently of a specific student teacher whom she had in sixth grade: "She taught me many things academically, yet I think she helped me grow as a person more. Within the weeks she attended our school she set up a group in which about eight of us girls would go talk. We had a lot of fun there, and we also learned a lot about ourselves and others. At this time in my school years we were still keeping journals. We would write whatever we wanted and the teacher would return it with a quick note. I would always hope that this woman would get my journal, and most of the time she did. After her first few days here she became more than a teacher, she became a positive role model, an idol, and more than that, a friend."

In addition to specific student teachers having an impact on the students, the activities these student teachers planned for their students were also appreciated and noted: "If I remember correctly each of my student teachers over the past few years have required us to do some sort of outside project. These projects have ranged from oral reports and collecting moss, to having a 'show and tell' day. All of the projects have been very enjoyable to work on. They were a little 'additive' to what we were doing."

The overall sense from students is that they do benefit from the contact with student teachers. Student teachers are seen to have a definite "additive effect" on the school experience of young adolescents.

University supervisor

University supervisors were nearly unanimous in agreeing that the student teacher's role was to assume gradually the responsibility for all teaching duties. The amount of full-time teaching in which the student teacher takes over the entire teaching load of the cooperating teacher depends on the site and the university supervisor. Several supervisors require at least two weeks of "total immersion" while others require more. Other activities include working with individual students, visiting special education placements, and observing other unique situations.

In describing the larger role and responsibilities of the "team" one university supervisor said: "The student teaching team is made up of the student teacher, the cooperating teacher, and the university supervisor. The cooperating teacher sets the framework within which the students will work, stating objectives and guiding the student teacher to achieve the most effective teaching for the benefit of the pupils. Through observing, assisting, planning, and teaching the student teacher learns to create a supportive learning environment for students and to recognize their individual differences. I believe the university supervisor serves as a facilitator who helps to assure the student teacher has every opportunity to reach his/her potential."

Supervisory techniques

Most university supervisors make weekly or biweekly visits to student teachers to observe at least one full class. Several report that they use a Hunter lesson plan model to evaluate student teachers, while others indicate they use the formative evaluation sheet available in that district. Most university supervisors attempt to conference with student teachers as soon after the observation as possible. One supervisor reports a pre-observation conference to discuss the lesson to be taught.

> While each student and cooperating teacher are encouraged to initiate a conference at any time, typically most conferences are initiated by the university supervisor. Sometimes the cooperating teacher is included and other times the university supervisor meets only with the student teacher, the composition being determined by the goal of the conference. Because of the time limitations and the natural tendency of students to expect such, I tend to direct the agenda. However, I try to be open and encouraging of whatever subject needs to be discussed. This is the time where strengths and weaknesses are informally assessed and goals and plans are set for continued growth. The growth which results naturally plays into the evaluation process.

Evaluation

University supervisors emphasize the collaborative nature of the evaluation process with student teachers, cooperating teachers, and university supervisors all playing key, if not equal, roles. One university supervisor described the role of evaluation.

> In the final analysis, evaluation of a student's performance at best is subjective, and sometimes almost subconsciously

a comparative process. I try to set up each student to succeed from the beginning and support that goal throughout by keeping the student's question of 'How am I doing?' updated, while encouraging the cooperating teacher and student to work together toward the goal of being an effective teacher. But most important in the evaluation process, I try to lead the student toward being able to evaluate his/her own performance, planning, etc., and to self-correct, for in the long run, that will serve the student teacher best.

Enhancing professional development

If student teaching is valuable for student teachers, it is also valuable for university supervisors. Often seen by their public schools counterparts as "removed from the action," university supervisors use their work with student teachers as a way to stay current with K-12 happenings. As one university supervisor said: "Each time an evaluation takes place it is an opportunity for me to question what are effective means of dealing with teachers and students in a classroom situation."

Other university supervisors were enthusiastic about student teaching supervision: "This experience keeps me constantly in touch with the realities and the demands of public school personnel and gives me insights into 'crying needs.'" Another says: "I am always energized when I am in the field, for it is there that I get excited by new programs and innovative teaching styles and the undying enthusiasm of some teachers. I enjoy talking to principals, teachers, and specialists. Sometimes I get discouraged by what I see and hear. But being in the schools helps to keep my learning process ongoing, enriching my experiential background so that I can be a more resourceful, effective supervisor, and can keep the 'practice' part of 'theory and practice' in perspective."

A Five Year Integrated Model

Jerry Moore
Tom Oppewal

The program description that follows details the major changes the University of Virginia has taken in their teacher education reform efforts, especially as these affect the preparation through field experiences at the middle level.

Our response to the challenges confronting teacher education began in the early 1980's. Public schools, which had previously provided laboratory settings for the traditional program of teacher education, joined with the Curry School of Education in the development of a collaborative program of field experiences for prospective teachers. A task force outlined a governance structure for the recruitment, identification, and appointment of a clinical faculty, a term used to describe practitioners who participate in medical education. Classroom teachers seeking to become clinical faculty apply for this position and these applications go through an extensive evaluation process by both school and university personnel.

The clinical faculty and teacher education faculty, after training, are jointly responsible for the supervisory triad. More important, clinical faculty participate directly in the teacher education program as teaching models, as supervisors, as teachers in the program, and as decision-makers regarding curriculum and instruction issues. One of the central beliefs for the new program is "that the professional field has joint responsibility with the university in the preparation of teachers."

The teacher education program is a five year program in which students take courses in both the College of Arts and Sciences and the Curry School of Education. In this new design, all students, regardless of the type of certification sought, must have an academic major and fulfill liberal arts core requirements like all other students in the university. Students that complete this integrated program receive a Bachelor of Arts degree from the College of Arts and Sciences and a Master's degree from the Curry School of Education.

The field sequence: A brief overview

The clinical experiences and the generic professional studies begin in the second year of the program and continue with course and field experience in each of the last eight semesters. Each course in the professional core is extended into field practice which acts to integrate knowledge and practice. Professional practice in the field largely shapes what the prospective teacher will choose for specialization. During the second year of the program all prospective teachers are assigned to an elementary or a middle school field experience regardless of their initial interests. We have found this to be the single best recruiter of college students interested in middle school teaching. Both elementary and secondary education students may choose to emphasize middle school through subsequent field experience.

Moving to the fifth year, students emphasize their level of specialization in which they will later seek employment through a teaching associateship. Early exposure to the middle grades and greater flexibility in delaying the decision regarding teacher placement have resulted in a significantly larger number of elementary and secondary education students choosing the middle grades for their teaching associateship experience.

The fifth year: Teaching associateship and field project

The sequence of field experiences in the fifth year includes the teaching associateship and the field project. The teaching associateship generally takes place in the fall semester of a student's fifth year in the teacher education program. Many of the teaching associateship experiences are composed of two seven week placements at two different schools. Students seeking elementary certification may be placed in a middle school for the first half of their teaching placement and an elementary or primary placement for the last half. Secondary students may be in a high school the first half of the teaching associateship and placed in a middle school the last half. In conjunction with the teaching associateship experience, a weekly seminar is held at various schools to address common concerns and problems that arise and to offer sessions on such topics as how to interview for a job and the certification process.

The field project is a field based research project—the culminating activity of the teacher education program. During their teaching associateship experience, students are asked to identify a problem or issue they are interested in studying. In the final semester of the program, each teacher candidate must design, conduct, and present a field project (action research) in response to that problem. The research project is more than just a library research paper. Students return to the schools where they did their student teaching to collect data. The clinical instructor serves as a resource person in helping the student gain access and to collect data. Many of these research questions are directly related to school problems that the teaching associate encountered while student teaching. Students who taught at the middle level have another opportunity to understand more fully the unique set of characteristics and problems that they will encounter when they begin their teaching careers.

Multiple Perspectives on the Teaching Associateship Experience

A university supervisor, clinical instructor, teaching associate, and young adolescent student were interviewed to generate the following discussion on the teaching associateship experience in the middle schools in and around Charlottesville, Virginia.

University supervisor

One semester before the teaching associateship begins, the university supervisor arranges a meeting with the various schools to discuss placements. This input, along with teaching associate requests for schools, grade level, and teachers, leads to their appropriate placement—a decision made by the Director of Teacher Education.

Prior to the teaching associateship, the university supervisor has a meeting with teaching associates to provide an overview of the experience. The university supervisor also sets up a meeting between clinical instructors, teaching associates, and building principals in order to discuss procedures, expectations, and guidelines. Teaching associates are encouraged to attend the first day of classes in order to meet students at the same time their clinical instructor meets the new class members.

During the teaching associateship experience, the university supervisor, with the clinical instructor's input, plans the student's program and evaluation. Whereas the clinical instructor assumes responsibility for day to day planning and supervision, the university supervisor is a resource person for more long-range planning.

The role of the university supervisor is to coordinate the conferencing and evaluation process with the teaching associate and the clinical instructor. The university supervisor makes at least one visit every two weeks to observe the teaching associate. Conferencing is done on the same day the lesson is observed and suggestions are made if improvement is needed. At two different times during the placement, the university supervisor conducts evaluations on the teaching associate's success in the areas of planning, classroom management, instruction, methodology, and professionalism. These evaluations are in written form and shared with both the clinical instructor and the teaching associate. The clinical instructor, in coordination with the university supervisor, follows a similar evaluation cycle.

The clinical instructor

The clinical instructor does not play a specific role in teaching associate placements. Placements are worked out between the university's teacher education office, the central office, and the building principals. Clinical instructors go through a rigorous selection and training process and are the only teachers that supervise teaching associates.

One clinical instructor who works in an urban middle school of six hundred students, said that once she knows which teaching associate will be assigned to her classroom, she makes every effort to make these persons feel a part of the school community. She encourages students to attend faculty meetings and "back to school night," and to meet the parents of classroom students. Teaching associates are also encouraged to sit with students at lunch, and supervise dismissal and bus duty. She believes teaching associates should be totally immersed in school life rather than just observing.

As a cooperating teacher, the clinical instructor expects teaching associates to have the skills and knowledge necessary to organize teaching units and to manage the classroom environment. Within several weeks, teaching associates are usually ready to take over all the classes and carry out the full responsibilities of the classroom teacher. The clinical instructor now acts as a resource person providing suggestions and assistance in classroom management techniques, use of materials, and teaching strategies. Conferencing at the end of each day enables the clinical instructor to give the teaching associate both written and verbal feedback on the day's activities. When a student has problems, the clinical instructor suggests alternative ways of approaching the problem.

Students are evaluated formatively in both written and verbal form. Summative evaluations are written by both the clinical instructor and the college supervisor. The student is given the opportunity to read and respond to the written summative evaluations.

One clinical instructor referred to herself as a "teaching associate junkie" because she always seeks them. She enjoys interacting with another adult in the classroom as well as the stimulation that comes from having someone watch how she manages and teaches her class. Teaching associates are resources for new teaching activities and unit ideas as well as a bridge between the latest research and the realities of the classroom. The personal and professional relationships that she develops contribute to her renewal as a teacher.

Participants

Sarah requested and received a middle school and elementary school placement, but did not choose the school nor the clinical instructor that worked with her. The split placement enabled her to have experiences at two levels of schooling, thus enabling her to make a more informed decision about which level of school she would like to teach.

The teaching associateship involves taking on most of the responsibilities of a classroom teacher. This job includes planning and delivering instruction, assessing student performance, and attending to all of the non-instructional tasks that encompass the teacher's role.

Some of the expectations placed on teaching associates originate from the teaching associates themselves. They strive to meet their own definition of a professional teacher. To Sarah this meant that she attend sporting and other after school intramural events. In addition to these expectations, the university supervisor and clinical instructor promote a number of behaviors and actions that each teaching associate is expected to meet. These include such things as maintaining the same contract hours as teachers, extra duties such as lunchroom supervision, teacher meetings, and tutoring children after school.

The teaching associate is not totally alone in her or his role because the clinical instructor and the university supervisor observe extensively and give both oral and written feedback in conferencing. Teacher LINK, an IBM sponsored project, facilitates communication between clinical instructor, teaching associate, and university instructor by way of portable computers.

The college supervisor generally completes a midterm and an end-of-term evaluation, and shares these written results with teaching associates. The clinical instructor also evaluates the teaching associate in similar fashion. Sarah evaluated both the clinical instructor and the university supervisor.

Adolescent student

Nathan described teaching associates as very nice, but they were not quite "real" teachers. He said they were somewhere between being real teachers and students still learning to be teachers. This meant he could tell the teaching associates things he would not mention to the classroom teacher. Though teaching associates teach classes and do many of the same activities as real teachers, they still are not thought of in the same way as the classroom teacher. The three teaching associates that were in Nathan's room during the year were described by Nathan as being friendly and easy to get to know. The teaching associates were all very different in how they acted in class and the way they taught. Nathan saw this as an advantage because he enjoyed getting to know different people and liked the variety they provided in the classroom.

Teaching associates were also perceived as a source of fun because they played lots of games with students and made learning enjoyable. Nathan was quick to point out that the classroom teacher did these things as well, but did not do them as often as the teaching associate. He also liked it when teaching associates brought resource people from the community in as guest speakers. One teacher brought in a speaker who had visited Alaska while another invited a local TV personality who came with an entire TV crew.

There were also some problems with having a teaching associate. For example, Nathan pointed out that is was difficult when the classroom teacher left the room. Sometimes he wanted to ask the classroom teacher for help and she was not around. Nathan thought if both his classroom teacher and teaching associate stayed in the room together, he would have the best of both worlds.

Summary

Ultimately, the clinical faculty program may well be the single, most significant part of the reform agenda at the University of Virginia. At the same time, we are still meeting the challenge that it initiated.

A Fifth Year Partnership Model

Cliff P. Bee
Linda Kramer

It is 7:30 Wednesday morning at La Mesa Middle School. The day has begun for a group of twenty San Diego State students as it has for 357 previous teacher education candidates. The classroom is filled with friendly conversation tinged with some anxiety, yet exuding great expectations of the day's events. For the next two hours these student teachers will participate in university classes, followed by time devoted to preparing for and teaching one class period at La Mesa. This routine is followed throughout the semester; a two-hour block of coursework is linked to a middle school teaching assignment.

The San Diego State-La Mesa Middle School Model is a unique student teaching model. Because it occurs as the first semester in a fifth year teacher education program, it is the teacher candidate's first "real" teaching experience. The pairing of this field placement with eight hours of university coursework in social foundations and educational psychology, both of which are conducted on site at La Mesa Middle School, makes for the kind of wholistic experience greatly appreciated by the program's participants. "The Block," as it is commonly denoted, stresses the integration of theory and practice not only through the combination of coursework with field placements, but also through the combined efforts of university professors and La Mesa teachers who work together as instructors in the program. This approach appears more meaningful and realistic for student teachers.

Development of the model

During the 1984 spring semester San Diego State University and the La Mesa-Spring Valley School District's La Mesa Middle School proposed a plan to improve the pedagogical skills of those who desired to enter the teaching profession. The underlying goal was to attract and train middle level teaching candidates, a difficult task because few teacher candidates identify the middle grades as their first teaching choice. Establishing an on site education program at a middle school seemed the logical way to introduce aspiring secondary teachers to the world of young adolescents. Under the guidance of Cliff Bee, a San Diego State professor, and the administration and teachers at La Mesa, a Partners in Education Committee (PIE Committee) was formed and the program begun.

Now in its seventh year, the program's strengths include:

1. The planning and implementation of both teacher education coursework and school site instructional strategies by university professors, teachers, and administrators.
2. The utilization of available research and professional experience in areas such as cooperative learning, peer coaching, clinical teaching/supervision, and middle school philosophy.
3. The use of experienced middle level teachers as instructors and guest speakers in university courses and as mentors in the student teaching experience.
4. The focus on cooperative decision-making among teacher candidates, teachers, administrators, and university professors.

Although the program has not received any special funding through grants or other soft dollars, its development has received encouragement and support from the surge of reform reports that have attempted to persuade universities to join forces with public schools. To date, the numbers of participants in the program have included 357 teacher candidates, 49 middle school faculty members, 13 school staff members, 12 school administrators, and 9 university faculty.

The La Mesa Middle School site

La Mesa Middle School was built in 1952 and is the oldest of the district's four middle schools. The building is designed with several classroom wings and specialty areas including computer labs, music classrooms and practice rooms, science labs, art rooms, and shop facilities. The school's current student enrollment is approximately 1,000, with 24% of the population ethnically diverse.

The school offers a transitional core curriculum with sixth graders having a four discipline core and seventh graders a two discipline core. The school is currently reorganizing to pilot interdisciplinary teams at the seventh and eighth grade levels. For instructional purposes, students are grouped both heterogeneously and homogeneously.

Context of the student teaching experience

At the beginning of the semester, college supervisors/instructors meet with La Mesa's administrators to share biographical information on all students who have signed up for the Block so that student teachers can be matched with the most appropriate master teacher and classroom setting. This information includes essays written by incoming student teachers, profiles of their related experiences with adolescents, and the coursework they have completed for subject matter specialization. Initial decisions about student teaching assignments are made at this time, but each decision is subject to the interest and approval of the master teacher (faculty member who supervises a student teacher). While we do place student teachers in other middle schools in the district using the same procedure, we attempt to place the majority of student teachers at La Mesa.

Background for student teaching

Before entering the Block, university students have completed degrees in their areas of specialization. In many cases they have been volunteers in schools or youth organizations, but in all cases they have completed 15 hours of observation in different kinds of schools. When they come to the program they have some knowledge of classroom life, and a great deal of knowledge about their subject areas. They are unsure about middle level students, and, to a large extent, picture themselves as high school teachers using instructional techniques similar to those of their professors.

One student teacher said: "I think when we first came here we had lots of different expectations about what we could expect from 7th and 8th graders in each of our subject areas. Those things went out the window."

In the La Mesa Block, however, university coursework is delivered by an interdisciplinary team with two university professors and one La Mesa faculty member assuming primary responsibility. No division is made between **Educational Psychology** and **Social Foundations**, and all assignments are given and evaluated collaboratively among instructors. Emphasis is placed on how student teachers can use this knowledge within their student teaching experiences at La Mesa.

During the first four weeks of the semester, the coursework consists of: (a) developing daily lesson plans and unit plans; (b) becoming familiar with instructional materials, state and district curriculum guides; and (c) classroom management. The focus is on theory and practicality. The La Mesa math teacher who is one of the three primary Block instructors describes it this way: "I think back to my own undergraduate methods courses and I swore

I'd never take another....Now I'm excited....There's a closer coordination here and greater practicality."

Various other La Mesa faculty members, administrators, and district personnel visit the class to talk about planning and management, and to share their own unique experiences. During this time the student teachers have received their classroom assignments and have begun observing the middle school students they will soon teach.

As the semester progresses, student teachers are required to complete three major assignments: (a) a curriculum unit plan; (b) a paper outlining the professional organizations and curriculum materials available in their fields; and (c) a curriculum/instruction project such as a game, learning center, or simulation. Student teachers receive feedback from their professors as well as their master teachers and, in some cases, from their own students, as they try their units and projects with real live subjects.

The importance of understanding the developmental characteristics of middle level students emerges frequently in Block discussions as student teachers test their project ideas. As the following comments from current and past student teachers indicate, this integration of coursework and practice makes lasting impressions.

"The curriculum unit plan was the most helpful thing. To plan and then do it kept us from the tendency to think about what we were doing today and what we're doing tomorrow, and got us to think about a unit of information that had to be communicated and understood."

"The one thing I sensed when I first came here was that this was a school that cared about us, and took it (teacher preparation) seriously. Here we were, novices and afraid to get up in front of everyone, and now...."

"Having district and school personnel invited into our university classroom really helps. Teachers lend listening ears in the lounges...and they smile at us and make us feel welcome. This is a positive experience here even though you're nervous about being evaluated."

The student teaching experience

The heart of the La Mesa Block Program is the student teaching experience itself. Usually by the fourth week of the semester each student teacher has assumed the responsibility for teaching one 50 minute class everyday until the public schools semester ends. Planning and delivering the content for this class is uppermost in the minds of our university students. In the beginning student teachers work closely with master teachers until, at the master teacher's discretion, they assume complete control of classroom events. The transition from observer to partial teacher and finally to full teacher is filled with anxiety and excitement. Student teachers are encouraged to bring their triumphs as well as their not-so-successful moments to share in the Block classes each morning. One student teacher explained it this way: "Having the Block gives us emotional support and academic support. We've gone through ups and downs (in teaching)."

The responsibilities of the various university and school-based personnel involved in student teacher supervision are highly structured, and, to a large extent, overseen by the school-based PIE Committee. The PIE Committee works together to make suggestions about experiences to which student teachers should be exposed, and to develop checklists for evaluation purposes. PIE members take on the responsibility of involving student teachers. As one master teacher explains: "Student teachers are part of the faculty as much as possible in social activities, in-services, and meetings. We want them to understand district policies and how they affect our schools."

Some of the activities arranged for student teachers by the Committee include: higher level thinking skills workshops, discipline, motivation, student test scores seminars, substitute teaching experiences, videotaping pre-conferences, lessons, and post-conferences.

Another master teacher comments: "This is extra work for our staff, but we benefit a great deal, too. We're dedicated to developing good student teachers."

Each student teacher is supervised by a university professor or graduate student who visits the student teacher's classroom once a week. The supervisors examine lesson plans and observe the teaching session, including pre- and post-conferences with the student teacher as often as possible. Supervisors, as well as master teachers, have been trained in clinical teaching, and their feedback to student teachers reflects this model. When university supervisors are not part of the Block faculty, they frequently attend the class to gain a general overview of student teachers' problems and concerns, and to schedule the weekly observations.

Student teachers receive constant feedback from master teachers, and formal, written evaluations twice during the semester. On these occasions, the student teacher, university supervisor, and master teacher meet together to share notes and observations. Noted one master teacher: "I feel I've benefited a great deal from this (having a student teacher). We sit together and brainstorm a lot, and when I see creative things I steal them! My bulletin boards have never looked better."

So dedicated is La Mesa Middle School to the notion of supervisory conferencing that the PIE Committee arranges a substitute teaching experience for student teachers. This activity frees other student teachers for additional, uninterrupted conference time with master teachers and supervisors.

A principal says there is "a collegial, collaborative program between our university and our school. I'm so pleased we're part of the effort, the way of life."

Professional development: A shared commitment

Speaking to the value of the program, one student teacher commented: "Being in this on site program makes you feel more like a part of the middle school, and you are around the kids more. It lets you get used to the system. It breaks you in so to speak."

Another student teacher echoed these thoughts: "Having an on site program gives us, student teachers, a realistic view of the lifestyle of the professional teacher. Interacting with middle school kids, teachers, administrators, and parents is good preparation...."

The La Mesa Middle School Block Program is one example of how schools and universities can work together to provide the best professional beginning for student teachers. We are especially pleased with the program because, at a time when California is attempting to restructure middle level schools, San Diego State is among the few universities here paying greater attention to future middle level teachers.

How can we be sure the program is effective? One outcome of the La Mesa Program is the number of pre-service teachers who begin the semester enjoying the middle school and young adolescents, too! A second indication is the warm welcome provided by La Mesa's faculty and administration. As active participants in the university coursework and supervision of student teachers, they ensure not only their own professional development but the development of their profession as well.

As professors, the daily opportunity to be on a middle school campus lends credence to the theories and skills we attempt to teach our university students. Being able to take advantage of the wide range of expertise offered by the La Mesa faculty and administration makes our program stronger and more fully alive. We hope the higher education presence on campus stimulates teachers to try new things and enables them to ask for assistance more easily. From providing in-service sessions to suggesting other university speakers, from bringing curriculum materials unavailable at the school, to teaching an occasional class of young adolescents ourselves, university professors find they are better able to practice the skills of this profession. The San Diego State-La Mesa Model makes the world of middle level professional preparation come alive for student teachers, master teachers, and professors alike.

Part IV

Building Effective Field Experience Programs

Questions and Responses

What are some of the key goals of middle level field experiences?

Field experiences provide settings for applying one's knowledge and skills, experiencing the complex interactions of learning environments, and integrating theory and practice. By bringing students as close as possible to the real world of the classroom, these experiences enhance understanding. Key goals of middle level field experiences include:

To understand the developmental characteristics of young adolescents;
To assist in career decision-making and placement at
    appropriate grade levels;
To apply learning theories and age appropriate instructional practices;
To develop systematic observation skills and reflective teaching
    practices;
To develop positive social interaction and communication skills;
To foster a disposition towards lifelong learning.

How should field experiences be structured?

Middle level field experiences need to begin early in teacher preparation and continue throughout the program. Each experience should include a clearly articulated focus with defined goals and objectives. Subsequent experiences should build upon prior ones and all need to reflect the knowledge base undergirding the program. As students progress through these field experiences, they should assume increasingly more of the teacher's roles and responsibilities. Thus, field experiences need to be an integral and cohesive part of the total teacher preparation program.

Field experiences also need to reflect the diversity of middle level organizational structures and programs. As students participate in school settings, they receive exposure to multiple middle grade organizational structures.

All field experiences should focus on the developmental characteristics of young adolescents and their implications for age appropriate education. These characteristics underpin the middle school concept and its translation into practice. Thus, field assignments need to continuously guide students in relating their experiences to young adolescents' developmental characteristics.

Throughout the field experiences, there needs to be a structure which encourages reflection and supports students. This structure can take many forms including on- or off-site seminars/courses conducted by university and/or school personnel. Student reflection promotes the integration of theory and practice. Supporting students during field experiences increases the likelihood of a successful experience. Creating cohort groups, teams or pairs of students in school settings also provides a peer support structure and offers multiple perspectives on interpreting experiences.

How do you assure active participation during field experiences?

The cooperative efforts of university faculty, cooperating teachers, and pre-service students can assure active participation. Structuring field experiences with explicit objectives and including assignments that require involvement are specific techniques to achieve this goal.

If designing the field experience is a collaborative effort between the university and middle level schools, its goals are more likely to be implemented. After clearly structuring the program, communicate it to cooperating teachers and pre-service students. Written guidelines, expectation checklists, and supervisory training all serve to effectively convey a program's goals.

Create a system for monitoring student involvement. Again, communication between all involved parties is critical. Student logs or journals provide input. Site visits by university personnel and joint conferences can monitor involvement and solve problems when necessary.

Design assignments/modules for students that require active participation. When doing this, keep in mind that active involvement takes overt and covert forms. If the student is cognitively interacting with the experience, that is active participation. Involving students in systematic and reflective observation, critical thinking, problem solving, or decision making all actively engage the learner. Create field experience requirements that balance overt and covert participation.

How do I assure that students are exposed to the middle school philosophy in practice?

When middle level schools that reflect the middle school philosophy are not accessible for field experiences, there are many ways to assure exposure to exemplary middle grades practices and structures. Locate an exemplary middle level school within driving distance and take your students on a field trip. If possible, visit several schools or the same school more than once.

Structure the field experience to focus on the developmental characteristics of young adolescents. Shadowing a young adolescent throughout a field experience provides considerable insight into the young adolescent's world. These understandings will guide the future teacher in better meeting young adolescents' needs.

Design a simulation that involves students in teaming, creating an "ideal" middle school or restructuring a middle level school. Collect videotapes of effective middle grades practices. You can make your own or use available tapes. One suggested tape is *Early Adolescence: A Time of Change—Implications for Schools* (National Middle School Association). Organize a conference call (with a speaker phone) between middle level teachers, principals, and pre-service students. This provides a question and answer forum for exploring middle level issues and concerns.

Establish a seminar that accompanies the field experience. In the seminar, provide a firm background in middle school philosophy and young adolescents' developmental characteristics. Throughout the experience, use this foundation as a basis for engaging in critical thinking exercises that examine how effectively observed schools meet developmental characteristics, thereby, comparing the real and the ideal (Butler & Dickinson, 1987).

Engage in professional behaviors that expose students to age-appropriate practices, such as attending state, regional and/or national middle level conferences, reading journals (*Middle School Journal, Journal of Early Adolescence*), or joining the National Collegiate Middle School Association (NCMSA, University of Northern Colorado, McKee Hall 208, Greeley, CO 80639).

Should students participate at one or multiple middle grade levels?

Experience at multiple middle grade levels provides a broader base for understanding the developmental dynamics of early adolescence and the implications for appropriate education. This exposes the future teacher to the range of developmental diversity. This exposure guides pre-service students in noting that diversity best describes middle level students both within and between grade levels. Middle level teachers will support the position that sixth graders behave differently from eighth graders. Participation at multiple middle grade levels also enables students to observe articulation with elementary and secondary programs and the continuum of organizational structures, e.g., self-contained classrooms, core programs, and interdisciplinary teams. In addition, placement in diverse middle grade sites, such as K-8 schools, intermediate, junior high or middle schools, heightens students' awareness of the variance in middle grade organizational structures.

Whether participation experiences occur at one or multiple middle grade levels is often influenced by the number and duration of field experiences in a program and state certification regulations. Regardless of these limitations/requirements, we best prepare students for effective middle level teaching by exposing them to the varied programs designed to meet the diverse needs of young adolescents.

If large numbers of students are observing in the field unsupervised, how can you maintain contact with teachers and these students?

Use self-addressed postcards which ask for the desired feedback from teachers, e.g., attendance, attitude, positive student interactions, etc. Students give the postcards to the teachers at the desired feedback intervals and teachers mail them back to the university supervisor.

Conduct an on-site conference with all involved teachers one or more times during the field experience. Hold late afternoon or evening seminar sessions for students to discuss their experiences.

Mail an introductory form letter which includes evaluation instruments specifying the return time frames. Include a self-addressed envelope(s). Collect journals periodically to track their visits (regularity and timing).

How do cooperating teachers assure that their initial contacts with students go well?

Since effective middle level teaching often requires "heroic" qualities, greet the pre-service student with the *EPIC* approach. Start with clear *expectations*. Share your expectations, preferably in writing. Specify the experiences/activities available in your classroom, professional conduct, school/class policies and regulations, a description of your role(s), and any other pertinent information. Reinforce the university's expectations. Solicit the student's expectations. Discuss the student's prior experiences in and out of school settings with young adolescents and any other information that assists in structuring the participation. In negotiating the nature of the experience, remember that each pre-service student is a unique individual and, therefore, your expectations need to be flexible enough to meet these diverse backgrounds and needs. Be *positive* and supportive. For many students, entering a middle school environment can be a scary experience. Remember your own initial years of teaching. Display enthusiasm for middle level teaching—it is contagious. *Involve* the student immediately. Expose the student to the multiple roles and responsibilities of middle level teachers. Engage the student in a representative balance of your typical activities. As the experience progresses, encourage increasing levels of involvement. Treat the student in a *collegial/collaborative* manner. Invite the student to take part in the role of teacher as decision-maker. If you are a member of a team, treat the student as an additional member. Added together, these set the tone for an *EPIC* experience.

What if university students arrive ill-prepared or with unprofessional behaviors?

Responses to a student arriving ill-prepared depend upon the nature and severity of the lack of preparedness. Two criteria assist in deciding if the student should continue in the experience. First, is the deficiency in preparation potentially harmful to the well-being of the young adolescents in the classroom? Secondly, does the field site offer opportunities to fill these gaps or are they better addressed in a university setting? Clearly articulating concerns to both the student and the university supervisor is essential. Collaboratively deciding on the most appropriate response given the circumstances follows.

An ounce of prevention can help avoid conflicts over inappropriate attire or behaviors. University supervisors should be informed of dress and behavioral expectations and other pertinent building policies. These also need to be conveyed to students in advance of their arrival at the field site. Create a clear policy, for example, that university students are expected to model their attire after the faculty/individual cooperating teacher. Stipulate consequences for failing to follow this policy. Remind them that modeling responsible behavior reinforces the development of self-responsibility in young adolescents. Individual counseling on these issues prior to beginning the field experience can help avoid conflicts.

How do you compensate cooperating teachers for participating?

Rewards/compensations should reflect the degree of involvement required of the cooperating teacher. The amount of contact with preservice students along with field experience responsibilities should coincide with the benefits given to teachers. Rewards/compensations can take tangible and intangible forms.

Integrating cooperating teachers fully into the field experience program by collaborating on program planning, delivery, and evaluation is one form of compensation. Collaborating with university faculty by exchanging classes, teaching seminars, or making presentations are intangible forms of reward. Simply acknowledging and recognizing cooperating teachers as professional colleagues is meaningful.

Giving cooperating teachers adjunct faculty appointments at the university, particularly if their names appear in the catalog, says much. Monetary compensation for services is certainly in order.

Publicly recognize and acknowledge teachers' contributions. Recognition may take many forms such as plaques posted at the university or placement sites, certificates of acknowledgement, or honorary dinners/ functions. Provide perks related to university functions such as tickets to sports and/or cultural events, campus parking benefits, tuition waivers, or offering on site free graduate courses.

References

Butler, D.A., & Dickinson, T.S. (1987). Learning the middle school concept through field based experiences. *Middle School Journal, 18*(4), 37-39.

Common Threads

Throughout this monograph readers have been treated to a range of middle level field experiences. Each of the various components, from early observation through student teaching, is currently in place in a college or university program. But these field experiences share more in common than the fact that they are part of the growing body of best practice. They also share other commonalities, commonalities that bind them together into a coherent whole. In effect, these middle grades field experiences are effective because they incorporate these threads.

Each model:

1. Is grounded in the developmental aspects of the young adolescent;
2. Has definable purpose;
3. Actively engages preservice teachers in real classroom experiences;
4. Links theory and practice through planned reflection;
5. Allows students to experience diversity—both in those they teach and in their instructional techniques;
6. Has instructors/supervisors that recognize the value of field experiences.

1. Developmental aspects

The foundation of middle level education as a whole and middle grades field experiences specifically is the developmental stage of early adolescence. In the early observation experience at Wabash College or the all-day shadow study at Georgia Southern University, students are directed toward the developmental diversity of this period of life. Engagement in the diversity of this stage, whether physical, intellectual, social, emotional or moral, is primary to all that follows. In all the field experiences examined here the focus is continually on the middle grades student.

2. Definable purpose

Purposeful behavior is a key goal of all levels and aspects of education. This is especially true of the field experiences profiled. What may best illustrate this common linkage among these experiences is what is not here. There is no randomness, no abrogation of responsibility, no lack of meaning or substance. Students are engaged with a definable aspect of young adolescent development or middle grades schooling. What they are to study, learn about, or practice, is clearly articulated for a specific outcome. Students at Appalachian State University, for instance, emerge from their intern experience with a clear understanding of interdisciplinary units and teaming. Student teachers at the University of Maine have a broad and rich understanding and experience with the range of students in the middle grades, not just one age level.

3. Real classroom experiences

One demand that all of these field experiences make on their participants is activity. Even where observation is involved, it is active observation. Other field experiences, such as the St. Cloud and San Diego State-La Mesa experiences, immerse students into a totality of engagement.

4. Planned reflection

These experiences demand that students reflect upon the meaning of their involvement. Reflection takes many forms—journals, papers, seminars, individual conferences—but all are aimed at teasing out meaning—meaning about students, learning, and especially about self.

5. Student and instructional diversity

Richness characterizes these experiences and this richness is planned. All aspects of these field experiences build upon previous experiences, both in classrooms and in the field. And this richness is further enhanced by the wide diversity of experiences to which students are exposed. Multiple models of instruction are provided. Engagement with students as tutors and in small and large groups is provided. Diversity is also provided by the numerous instructors—college and university and public school teachers—that students engage with.

6. Supervision

When field experiences prove to be valuable, then those that oversee them treat them accordingly. Dedicated professionals in higher education and on site in schools devote considerable time, talent, and energy to these field experiences. The reward for these individuals, as for all of us, is a continuing cadre of highly trained and committed middle grades professionals.

Building a college or university middle level preparation program is a difficult task. One element that makes the task worthwhile is the linkage with middle level schools. Being *on site* is a critical aspect of effective middle level teacher education. The experiences outlined here are but a few of the ways that middle level teacher educators are preparing the next generation of middle school teachers. They are enough, however, to make it evident that much can and is being done to eliminate the lack of specially prepared middle level teachers that has plagued the movement too long.

PUBLICATIONS
National Middle School Association
(See 1991 Resource Catalog for member prices)

**On Site: Preparing Middle Level Teachers Through
Field Experiences** Deborah A. Butler, Mary A. Davies, and
Thomas S. Dickinson (84 pages) $8.00

As I See It John H. Lounsbury (112 pages) $12.00

The Team Process: A Handbook for Teachers
Third and enlarged edition
Elliot Y. Merenbloom (173 pages) $15.00

We Who Laugh, Last Julia T. Thomason and Walt Grebing
(64 pages) $6.00

**Life Stories: The Struggle for Freedom and Equality
in America** Lynn L. Mortensen, Editor (166 pages) $15.00

**Education in the Middle Grades: Overview of
National Practices and Trends**
Joyce L. Epstein and Douglas J. Mac Iver (92 pages)................ $12.00

**Middle Level Programs and Practices in the K-8
Elementary School: Report of a National Study**
C. Kenneth McEwin and William M. Alexander (46 pages) $8.00

A Middle School Curriculum: From Rhetoric to Reality
James A. Beane (84 pages) $8.00

**Visions of Teaching and Learning: Eighty Exemplary
Middle Level Projects** John Arnold, Editor (160 pages) $12.00

The New American Family and the School
J. Howard Johnston (48 pages) $6.00

**Who They Are—How We Teach: Early Adolescents
and Their Teachers**
C. Kenneth McEwin and Julia T. Thomason (26 pages) $4.00

The Japanese Junior High School: A View from the Inside
Paul S. George (56 pages) $5.00

Schools in the Middle: Status and Progress
William M. Alexander and C. Kenneth McEwin (112 pages) $10.00

A Journey Through Time: A Chronology of
Middle Level Resources Edward J. Lawton (36 pages) $5.00

Dynamite in the Classroom: A How-To Handbook for Teachers
Sandra L. Schurr (272 pages) $15.00

Developing Effective Middle Schools Through Faculty
Participation, Second and enlarged Edition
Elliot Y. Merenbloom (122 pages) $8.50

Preparing to Teach in Middle Level Schools
William M. Alexander and C. Kenneth McEwin (64 pages) $7.00

Guidance in Middle Level Schools: Everyone's Responsibility
Claire Cole (31 pages) $5.00

Young Adolescent Development and School Practices:
Promoting Harmony
John Van Hoose and David Strahan (68 pages) $7.00

When the Kids Come First: Enhancing Self-Esteem
James A. Beane and Richard P. Lipka (96 pages) $8.00

Interdisiciplinary Teaching: Why and How
Gordon F. Vars (56 pages) $6.00

Cognitive Matched Instruction in Action
Esther Fusco and Associates (36 pages) $5.00

The Middle School Donald H. Eichhorn (128 pages) $6.00

Long-Term Teacher-Student Relationships:
A Middle School Case Study Paul George (30 pages) $4.00

Positive Discipline: A Pocketful of Ideas
William Purkey and David Strahan (56 pages) $8.00

Teachers as Inquirers: Strategies for Learning With and About Early Adolescents Chris Stevenson (52 pages) $7.00

What Research Says to the Middle Level Practitioner
J. Howard Johnston and Glenn C. Markle (112 pages) $9.00

Evidence for the Middle School
Paul George and Lynn Oldaker (52 pages) $6.00

Involving Parents in Middle Level Education
John W. Myers (52 pages) $6.00

Perspectives: Middle Level Education
John H. Lounsbury, Editor (190 pages) $10.00

This We Believe NMSA Committee (24 pages) $3.50

Teacher to Teacher Nancy Doda (64 pages) $6.00

Early Adolescence: A Time of Change-Implications for Schools
Videocassette (37 minutes) $75.00

Early Adolescence: A Time of Change-Implications for Parents
Videocassette (50 minutes) $80.00

National Middle School Association
4807 Evanswood Drive
Columbus, Ohio 43229-6292

(614) 848-8211
FAX (614) 848-4301